Joseph Allen Costello

The Siwas - Their Life, Legends and Tales

Joseph Allen Costello

The Siwas - Their Life, Legends and Tales

ISBN/EAN: 9783337071561

Printed in Europe, USA, Canada, Australia, Japan

Cover: Foto ©Thomas Meinert / pixelio.de

More available books at **www.hansebooks.com**

THE SIWASH

THEIR

LIFE LEGENDS AND TALES

PUGET SOUND AND PACIFIC NORTHWEST

FULLY ILLUSTRATED

BY J. A. COSTELLO

SEATTLE
THE CALVERT COMPANY
716 FRONT STREET
1895

PREFACE

The excuse for this book is that it is the first attempt to depict the life or ethnology of the maze of Indian tribes on Puget Sound, and it is believed, will be found not wholly uninteresting. It has been the aim to attain as nearly the facts in every instance as possible which in any way lead to a proper understanding of the natives of the country as they were found by the first whites to arrive. Mika mam-ook mika tum-tum de-late wa-wa. Ko-pet mika ip-soot halo mika tum-tum ko-pa o-coke. De-late wa-wa mika tum-tum, nan-ich Sahg-a-lie Tyee; my heart speaks truthful and I hide nothing I know concerning the things of which I speak. My talk is truthful as God sees me.

From the old pioneer and the more intelligent native have all the material facts been drawn, and as these opportunities will not endure for many years longer it is the belief and hope that this work will find an enduring place in the home and public libraries.

For material aid in the compilation of the historical and pictorial matter of this work the author is indebted to Samuel F. Coombs, one of the few pioneers who has a genuine interest in the preservation of the life and habits and traditions of the aboriginees; H. A. Smith, of Smith's cove; Rev. Myron Eels for valuable information and assistance, touching the Skokomish Indians; Edward Morse, son of Eldridge Morse, than whom, probably none have a truer insight into the mysteries of early Indian life on the Sound; E. H. Brown, and to W. S. Phillips, F. Leather and Raphael Coombs, artists.

SEATTLE, December 14, 1895.

CONTENTS

LIST OF ILLUSTRATIONS

THE SIWASH

CHAPTER I

Early explorations of the Northwest coast now embraced in the limits of the state of Washington came after the discovery and occupation of the coast further south. Unlike the Mexican and California conquests it was devoid of wild and extravagant fact or fancy. There is found in the old annals no mention of barbaric splendor, no great empires or extensive cities, no magnificent spoils to be carried away.

The Spaniards first laid claim to the island of Vancouver in 1774. During the war of the Revolution, when England was occupied with her rebellious subjects on the Atlantic sea board, Perez Heceta and other Spanish navigators, explored and took possession, in the name of their sovereign, of the largest island on the Pacific coast.

What is now the straits of Juan de Fuca, or at that time Anian, had been explored by trading vessels from Spanish settlements along the Mexican coast, and doubtless by navigators of other nationalities, but it was not until near the close of the eighteenth century that the Northwest coast became disputed territory between Spaniards, English, Russians and Americans. In 1688, Martinez and Haro were dispatched by the government to the Pacific Northwest, to guard their newly claimed possessions, and here in the following year, Martinez seized a couple of English craft and immediately embroiled his parental country in a serious dispute with Great Britain. This was the initial movement in that spirited competition between the two rival nations which only ended when the Spaniards finally succumbed to British diplomacy and betook themselves to their southern possessions.

Captain Cook, the English navigator, who later fell a victim to the savage inhabitants of the Sandwich islands, was sent over by his government a few years after the Spanish occupation of the island, to discover, if possible a northwest passage which should unite the widely separated waters of the Atlantic and Pacific.   Cook perpetuated the memory of this voyage by giving names to a number of capes and promontories, chief of which is Cape Flattery.   At that time the waters of Fuca strait, Puget Sound and lands adjoining had not been christened by those names by which they are now known.

English navigators explored and gave names to Queen Charlotte islands and the surrounding waters soon after the occupation of the larger island of Vancouver, but they appear not to have visited the waters of the Georgian gulf until some years afterwards.

Numbers of navigators sent out by English companies visited the Northwest coast prior to the voyage of Captain Cook in 1785, and he, in succeeding years by many others who followed close upon his heels, giving names to and exploring channels and passages on the west side of Vancouver island.   Among the latter navigators who visited the country from 1785 to the close of the Eighteenth century were Captain Portlock in the ship King George, the ship Queen Charlotte, Captain Dixon, the latter naming the Queen Charlotte islands, Dixon strait, etc.   Then there was the Imperial Eagle, Captain Barclay, who sailed into the waters of Barclay sound, since which they have perpetuated the name of the worthy captain.   Captain Barclay sailed into the mouth of Fuca straits and sent a boat out on a short exploring expedition.   He then passed on south of Cape Flattery, where he had the misfortune to lose a boat's crew at the hands of the savages.   Captain Meares came the following summer, visited Clayoquot sound, gave the name to Fuca straits, christened Tatoosh island, and sailed along the coast southward to Shoalwater and Deception bays, and on to Cape Lookout, and thence retraced his steps to Barclay sound.   While here an exploring party of twelve men under First Officer Duffin were attacked by the Indians and beat a hasty retreat to the ship, after being severely wounded.   The vessel soon after returned to Nootka sound, where the ship Iphigenia, Captain Douglas, and the sloop Washington had arrived, followed soon after by the Columbia, Captain Kendrick, from Boston.   A new vessel had been built at Nootka during that year, and was christened Northwest America, which sailed soon afterwards, accompanied by the Iphigenia and Felice.

Captain Gray, of the Washington, wintered on the west coast of Vancouver island in 1788, and the following year circumnavigated the island, explored the west coast of Queen Charlotte island and called it Washington island.   He had, also, during this winter, a residence at Clayognut harbor.   Captain Gray built a fortification, and launched a small vessel, which he sent to Queen Charlotte island, previous to his sailing for the Atlantic coast.   George Vancouver did not come till 1792.

Soon afterwards Gray took command of the Columbia, sailed away for Boston and returned on a second voyage, and entered and named the Columbia river.

Captains Lewis and Clark explored the interior of Washington territory during Jefferson's presidency and settlements were made by the Hudsons Bay Company in 1828. The renowned Whitman came in the 30's to the Walla Walla country and Americans began to settle in 1845 on this side, then a part of the Oregon territory.

The name Puget Sound, as given by Vancouver, the British navigator, in 1792 extended only to the waters south of Point Defiance, near Tacoma. The waters north of this point were named Hood's canal, Admiralty inlet, Possession sound, Rosario straits, Gulf of Georgia, etc.

The name Puget Sound afterwards was applied to all the waters included in the American possessions south of British Columbia.

The Greek pilot Juan de Fuca is supposed to be the first man who ever sailed into these placid waters. He thought he had at last found the " Northwest Passage," but finding that such was not the case, he took possession of the country in the name of the king of Spain and then made his way back to Mexico. The straits of Fuca are about 12 miles in width and 100 miles long from its beginning to where it is lost in the many bays and fjiords and waters that surround the numerous islands at its head. There is perhaps no body of water that is as secure for the navigator as the straits of Juan de Fuca, there being no rocks or shoals in it. These northern waters are filled with numerous islands and the character of the country is almost the same from the 47th to the 60th parallel.

CHAPTER II

Oregon was the name given to the country west of the Rocky mountains and thought to extend to 54 degrees 40 minutes north. England also claimed the entire territory. In 1827 a treaty of joint occupation was formed, terminated in 1846 by the United States and it seemed for a time likely to embroil the two countries in war. A compromise was however effected fixing the international boundary at the 49th parallel, and through the good offices of the German Emperor, the beautiful San Juan islands were at last given to the American government. It had been said in the English parliament, by Sir Robert Peel: "England knows her rights and dares maintain them;" while Wentworth, of Illinois, in a speech before congress in January, 1844 said: "I think it our duty to speak freely and candidly and let England know that she can never have an inch of the country claimed as a part of the United States." Such is in brief the history of Washington prior to the actual occupation and settlement along in the latter 40's and the early 50's. Of these we shall speak more fully.

Many yet living within her borders and enjoying the benefits of mature and full-fledged statehood remember the time when Washington was an almost unexplored wilderness, silent and tomblike as the Sphinx. The first faint echoes of civilization were heard only along the shorelines of its inland sea, or along the water course of its debouching rivers. The vast and wealth-laden interior was unknown, the inner secrets of the Dark Continent today being perhaps better known than was the heart of this then northwestern territory. Ships of sail on occasional voyages ploughed the waters of the placid Sound, distributing here and there along the deeply wooded shore lines a pioneer with his family and rude effects, while the less majestic, though none the less important white-winged "Prairie" schooner, via the Willamette and the Rocky Mountain passes brought his neighbor, perhaps of Yankeedom, to keep him company in the wilderness. Suffering from the agonies of long sea voyages, or racked with the ills and tribulations of long overland journeys across burning sands and rocky passes, they pitched their rude habitations here in the primeval wilds to become neighbors of the dusky red man for many years while waiting for the population which should follow in their wake.

It was early in the forties when this onward march of civilization began landing in this country. 'Tis true the fur gatherer was here before them, but they were only transients and saw not, nor cared for the great natural wealth of the country that spread out before them.

In the Sound country, Fort Steilacoom, Port Townsend, Olympia and Seattle and a few down Sound ports became the central points of the sparse settlements which thus early began to spread over the country. The buzz of the saw mill was simultaneous with the first efforts of these early settlers, and in its wake came one of the most potent factors in the development of new countries—the newspaper.

As it was in California, so it was in a great measure in this northwest country, the greed for gold formed the incentive that hastened the early and quick settlement of the Northwest coast. "To Frazer River," was the watchword from California and the east, and thousands hastened to the unexplored country to find first, disappointment, and secondly, permanent homes. The overflow from the mines added many hundreds to the permanent settlements on the Sound and in the interior and the march of civilization and commerce was greatly augmented.

In 1858, and even at an earlier date, the newspaper became an important factor in the development of the country. On the 12th of March of that year, the first issue of the Puget Sound Herald appeared. The editor thereof, Mr. Charles Prosch, has humorously written of the manner in which he gathered in the $20-gold-pieces from enthusiastic subscribers, and speaks of his reception by the hardy settlers as having been exceedingly gratifying and flattering. At that time but one other newspaper was issued in the territory, that being the Pioneer and Democrat, a partisan journal of bitter proclivities.

Previous to 1845, this magnificent arm of the Pacific ocean—Puget Sound— was used only as a thoroughfare of trade by the Hudsons Bay company, and save the arrival of a few vessels in that company's service, its placid water was disturbed only by the canoe of the native red man, and the unbroken silence of the tree-clad shores proclaimed the country a wilderness. The posts of the above named company at Cowlitz river and Fort Nisqually were the only evidences of civilization. No extensive explorations had ever been made by the company's agents, and the Indians confined themselves to the streams and shores of the Sound and so gave no information regarding the country in the interior.

CHAPTER III

In August 1845 Col. M. T. Simmons, George Wauch and seven others arrived at Budd's inlet, under the pilotage of Peter Bercier, the first American citizens who ever settled north of the Columbia river. Being pleased with the appearance of the country Col. Simmons returned to the Columbia where he had left his family and in October of the same year moved over accompanied by J. McAllister, D. Kindred, Gabriel Jones, Geo. Bush and families, and J. Ferguson and S. B. Crocket, single men. They at first settled on prairies from one to eight miles back of the present town of Olympia.

They were fifteen days in completing this journey from Cowlitz landing to the Sound, a distance of 60 miles, being compelled to cut a trail through the timbered part of the country.

In the fall of the same year J. R. Jackson located at Aurora.

In 1846 S. S. Ford and J. Borst settled on the Chickeeles river, Packwood and Eaton with their families also joined the American settlers on the Sound the same year and Col. Simmons erected the first American grist mill north of the Columbia river. Previous to this the inhabitants had to subsist on boiled wheat or do their grinding with hand mills.

In 1847 the first house, a log cabin, was built in Olympia and E. Sylvester, Chambers, Brail and Shayer located on the Sound during the same year. The first saw mill was erected at the falls of Deschutes river by Col. Simmons and his friends during the same year. In June 1848 the Rev. Father Richard established the Roman Catholic mission of St. Joseph on Budd's inlet, one mile and a half below Olympia, and a few more families were added to the settlement of the Sound country that year.

In the year 1849 the brig Orbit from San Francisco put into Budd's inlet for a load of piles and that was the opening of the lumber trade.

In 1850 the first frame house was put up in Olympia, and during the same year Col. I. N. Eby made a settlement on Whidby island and a number of other improvements and new settlements were made during the year. In 1851 Fort Steilacoom was established by Capt. L. Balch, and Bachelor, Plummer, Pettygrove, Hastings and Wilson, names familiar even at this day around Port Townsend, came in the same year, while Steilacoom City by J. B. Chapman and New York (Alki point) by Mr. Lowe were founded.

From the beginning of the 50's the settlement of the country became too swift to permit of following the individual pioneers in their brave and daring exploits in hewing homes out of the primeval wilderness. There was no general way of reaching Puget Sound up to this time except by the toilsome trail from the Columbia river, and the necessity of a steamer from San Francisco became the leading topic in the settlements. Capt. A. B. Gove of the ship Pacific took the matter up and agitation, as it always does, soon after had the desired effect.

The report of Wilke's expedition and the development of the fur trade caused American interests to be directed toward this country. The account of Joe Meek who went overland from Walla Walla and gave such glowing descriptions of the Territory of Oregon had its effect, 1848, as he expressed himself; "this was the finest country that ever a bird flew over."

The lower house of Congress passed a bill to establish a territorial government for Oregon January 10, 1847, but many difficulties were in the way before it became a law, and the slave question, 1848, had its influence. It was in the middle of August of the last year of President Polk's administration before the territorial government bill for Oregon became a law and the long journey over the mountains caused much more delay.

Joseph Lane of Indiana was appointed Oregon's first Governor with Knitzing Pritchett of Pennsylvania as Secretary, W. P. Bryant of Indiana as Chief Justice, F. Turney of Illinois and P. H. Burnett of Oregon as Associate Justices, I. W. R. Bromley of New York as United States Attorney, Joseph L. Meek Marshal and John Adair of Kentucky Collector of the District of Oregon. Turney declining, O. C. Pratt of Ohio was named in his place. Bromley also declined and Amory Holbrook was appointed in his place. The party landed at Oregon City two days before the expiration of Polk's term of office.

During the fall of 1852 the people of Northern Oregon, now Washington, were loud in their demands for a separate territory and The Columbian, a bright little paper published at Olympia, became a zealous worker in behalf of a separate jurisdiction.

Northern Oregon was at first slow to attract the full tide of emigration, the worn out travelers who had journeyed across the plains were glad to find a resting place in the valleys of the Columbia or Willamette and those people who had homes established in Southern Oregon were always eager to discourage the emigration to the northern territory and often circulated reports condemning the Puget Sound country that caused a degree of enmity to exist between the two sections of the Northwest. The majority of the population being south of the Columbia river had the result of causing the attention of the government to be always directed to that part of the country and every appropriation from Congress was for the benefit of Southern Oregon and for a time the country bordering on Puget Sound was left to take care of itself. That naturally caused the people who had sought homes in that northern part of the country to ask that they be formed into a separate territory.

Not among the least of the trials and dangers which beset the early pioneer, were those which arose by reason of the contact with Indians. The average Siwash was a peaceable being, but the worst danger came from the deceitful and savage northern tribes and east of the mountain clans. From Nootka sound, Queen Charlotte and Vancouver islands, came swarms of the red devils in their nimble canoes and left havoc and destruction among many a pleasant home and settlement. Across the Cascade passes came bands of painted warriors spreading terror and death on every side.

Numbers of the early settlers fell early victims to the atrocities of these bloodthirsty bands, and their names are only remembered by the few survivors whose silver hair and wrinkled features form objects of interest, as they stand upon the pavement, in the pushing throng now crowding our busy thoroughfares. If you will ask Charles Prosch, Hillory Butler, Judge Swan, John Collins, G. A. Meigs and other old patriarchs yet among us, they can recount many a stirring tale of battle and ambush, and name over many an old settler who years ago gave away his life in his efforts to pave the way for the thousands, who, happy in the peaceful present, go about their daily work with scarce a thought of those early times.

Concerning themselves the rightful owners of the soil, the Indians, looked with jealous eye upon the daily encroachment of the whites and regarded with increasing and ominous distrust the oft repeated and oft broken promises held out to them that this land would be purchased under treaties with the government. Then the habits of the Indian was disgusting to the eye of civilization and no language can ever draw the slothful and dirtyness of this people, yet there were many wrongs done them and it was no more than could be expected that they would, true to their nature, do such acts of barbarity as would shock the whites and bring upon the Indian a terrible revenge and that a war for supremacy would only end in his discomfiture.

"Money was plentiful," remarks one of the early chroniclers of those times, "and I was not a little surprised at the abundance of money in the hands of the people. All but the farmers seemed to carry purses well filled with twenty dollar gold pieces. The farmers had been driven from their homes and impoverished by the Indian wars of 1856, from the effects of which they had not had time to recover ; but the men engaged in cutting piles and logging for the mills (and they comprised a large proportion of the whites here) suffered but little from the same cause. The man who owned the building in which I first printed my paper could neither read nor write, but managed to earn thirty dollars a day by hauling piles with three yoke of oxen from the timber to the water. Soldiers received permission from the officers to cut these piles, and earned ten dollars each a day. All lumbermen were paid in like manner.''

The now historic Hudsons Bay company was in early Washington days a power in the wilderness and with the native Indians. Their agents and trappers encroached upon every square mile of wilderness, almost from Hudsons bay to Puget Sound. Their forts occupied the most important places in the developing Northwest, and were viewed with more or less of distrust by American settlers. Fortunately, a friendly and parental government intervened in time, to the great advantage of the pioneers dwelling upon the disputed country. First a ten years' lease of, and then final purchase of the improvements of the Hudsons Bay company did away forever with the English fur monopoly in Washington territory.

In 1858 the permanent white settlement on Puget Sound numbered, according to one chronologer, 2500. The festive boomer in real estate and the dispenser of town lots and "wildcat" schemes was a being incognito. His sun had not then risen. A single newcomer in those times was an event of neighborhood notoriety. The blowing of an incoming steamer's whistle was a signal for every resident, male, female, child and Indian to hasten to the landing, the former to peer into the faces of the passengers for friends or relatives, the latter to gape in open-eyed astonishment at the white man's monster, the steamboat.

CHAPTER IV

THE SIWASH CHARACTERISTICS

The history of the Siwash is tradition, as it is with all aborigines. The early tales of the Norsemen, the Gaul, the Celt, are mere matters of history, perhaps distorted, but withal, history. The lower the order of the race, the lower its mental capacities, the more truth there is in the lore—the tales of its past. The incidents of their lives which collectively become their history, are handed down from father to son, from generation to generation, plain and unembellished. The Siwash, a race to whom instinct is superior to thought, are perhaps the strongest example of a people whose history is least faulty. What grandsire has told to father is retold to son in a language whose vocabulary is so limited as not to permit of changing of the original subject matter. True, the same deficiency of mental power blots out the distant past. Three generations represent the era of their history; beyond that the grandsire's memory closes; but as the incidents which are here chronicled are within the memory of many natives living at this time, and from whom they were gathered and related without variation it can be truly accepted as authentic. It has been practically accepted as a historic fact that Vancouver first penetrated into Puget Sound with his vessel the Discoveror. Juan de Fuca preceded him on the straits, but to Vancouver belongs the glory of having first penetrated to the upper Sound and pointed out a way for the sturdy pioneers that were to follow him. The first vessel of which the Indians, on the upper Sound at least, had any memory at the time the whites began to flock among them was certainly Vancouver's.

TYPICAL SIWASH FACE

The Siwash of Puget Sound (a general term applied to males of all the tribes) and the Indians of the entire North Pacific coast, like every native of every country possessing significant features of topography, flora, and most of all climate, is bent to his surroundings. The Siwash is the creature of the circumstances of climate in a very great degree, and he could never escape it—never will till the last of his race is lost in oblivion. His mode of life, the almost continual living in a squatting, cramped position in his canim from generation to generation, shows in his broken, ungraceful proportions today; and it cannot be doubted but that in the humid atmosphere of Puget Sound and the abreviated territory in which he has lived are to be found the potent factors that have united to make him at this day the essence of ugliness in human mould.

No matter where the Siwash came from, his past is so remote it will never be known.

A favorite way some have and a plausible excuse for saying anything at all, is to speculate on the Asiatic origin of the Indians of this part of America. Captain Maryatt tries to locate the Shoshones, whom he gives very wide latitude and longitude on the Pacific coast, among ruined cities and an extinct civilization and fauna, in distant Tartary; the Hydias are ascribed to Japan; the Kanacka resembles the Japanese, etc. As well assume the Siwash of Puget Sound are descendants of the Dakotahs or of some of the tribes east of the great Father of Waters, because the Thunderbird myth is traced from east to west with slightly

A KLOOTCHMAN

varying antecedents and forms from one tribe to another. The Indian origin is a theme for speculation only.

The Siwash is indubitably the result of hundreds of years residence on the forest-fringed shores of his Whulge. He probably could not endure for a generation elsewhere. He is completely moulded to his surroundings and is more nearly able to resist the deleterious results of the superior civilization than 99 out of 100 of the tribes in the broad interior of the American continent. Years and years ago, when the renowned old Chief Sealth was at the head of the allied tribes around Sdze-Sdze-la-lich and Squ-ducks (Seattle and West Seattle, or Elliott bay and Alki point), it is said that his legions numbered not more than 750 or 800 Indians. Who today will say that there is not now nearly that number of Indians almost within the same confines? In the face of the most aggressive development and civilization of the last ten years, robbed of every favorite haunt for hunting and fishing, with paddle wheels never ceasing to disturb the quiet waters of his ancient rivers and bays where the salmon was wont to sport, and with new population that had encroached upon every foot of land where his klootchman might have raised a little patch of potatoes, as she did a score of years ago, he has withstood it all and continues to hold on. No one ever hears of a Siwash dying unless occasionally on the reservations. A papoose dies once in a while during a change from the ordinary modes of life brought about by annual migrations to the hop fields.

The Siwash is the very reverse of a Nomad. He is studious only in his stolidity and inactivity. He never travels within the meaning of the word, and there's probably not a dozen of the full-blooded Indians who have been fifty miles from salt water. It was not infrequent for the plains' Indians beyond the great coast range of mountains to descend to the sea, but that the Siwash should ascend to and beyond the summit of those lofty and snow-clad hills— never.

Out of his canoe he is a fish out of water, a sloth away from his natural surroundings. He is like a seal on shore, a duck on dry land, ungainly and awkward. He never, probably, was brave, never quarrelsome in that he went out in search of war. Not infrequently he was the object of forays by his kinsmen from the far north or the east. Then he defended himself and family as best he could and got into the brush with all possible haste, where he was as safe from pursuit as if in a citadel. Not in the museums anywhere in the country is there at this time, it is believed, a single genuine implement of war of the early Indians who lived on the shores of Puget Sound. The Atlantic seaboard and the interior were deluged with centuries, it may be said, of savage warfare. One short war, a mere uprising on Puget Sound in early days, and that instigated by natives living beyond the edges of the Puget Sound forest, and all was over. Ever after the Siwash was an indifferent, uncomplaining creature. He drew one or two short annuities and government aid was practically withdrawn, and that, too, after his heritage of woods and waters had been taken from him. But one hears no plaint of disturbed and unmanageable Indians. He is content to live on so long as there is space for his cedar canoe to glide on the water and an open beach whereon he may erect a temporary tent.

LA BELLE KLOOTCHMAM

CHAPTER V

The Puget Sound Indians have generally been classified according to the language spoken by them in the Selish family or Flathead group. They were first classified in this way by Albert Gallatin, who was one of the first Americans to interest himself in the ethnology of the North American Indian. The extent of the Selish family was not known by Gallatin, neither did he know the exact locality of the tribe whose name he extended to this great family of tribes. The tribe is stated to have resided upon one of the branches of the Columbia river, which must be either the most southerly branch of Clark's Fork or the most northerly branch of Lewis river. The former supposition is correct. As employed by Gallatin the family embraced only a single tribe, the Flathead tribe proper. The Atnah, a Selishan tribe was considered by Gallatin to be distinct, and the name Atnah according to him would be eligible as the family name ; preference, however, is given to Selish. The few words given by Gallatin in his American Archæology from the Friendly Village near the sources of the Salmon river belong under this family.

Since Gallatin's time our knowledge of the territorial limits of this great linguistic family has greatly extended. The most southerly tribes are the Tillamooks who extend along the Oregon coast about 50 miles south of the Columbia river. Beginning on the north side of Shoalwater bay, Selishan tribes held the entire northwestern part of Washington, including the whole Puget Sound region except some insignificant spots about Cape Flattery, which were held by the Makah and the Chimakuan tribes. The Selishans also held a large portion of the eastern coast of Vancouver island, while the greater area of their territory lay on the main land opposite and included much of the country tributary to the upper Columbia. They were hemmed in on the south mainly by the Shahaptian tribes. They dwelt as far east as the extreme eastern feeders of the Columbia, and on the southeast their territory extended into Montana.

Within the territory thus indicated there are a great variety of costumes with greater differences in language.

During the early explorations along the Pacific coast the Selishan Indians held the territory along the western coast of Vancouver island as far north as Nootka sound, but since that time the Aht races of the west coast of the island have crowded them to the southward and eastward until now even the Neah bay agency is largely composed of Makah Indians, while the Chimakuans have obtained a strong foothold further south along the coast.

These Selish Indians were subdivided into numerous tribes, each one speaking a language a little different than the rest.

The Semi-ah-moos occupied the region of country nearest the British boundary line, but they were not a large tribe.

Proceeding southward were the Nooksacks, who inhabited the valley of the river of the same name; the Lummies, who lived around Bellingham bay; the Samish Indians, who camped along the banks of the Samish river and around its mouth, while the more important tribes to the south of them were the Skagits, Snoqualmies, Nis-qual-lies and Puyallups. On the west side of the Sound the most important tribes were the Chehalis, Clallam, Cowlitz, Sko-ko-mish or Twanas and Chinook Indians.

The Snoqualmies occupied the valleys of the Snohomish and Snoqualmie rivers from a short distance above the mouth of the Snohomish. The Snohomish Indians proper lived around its mouth. Much of the time the Snoqualmies occupied a large portion of the Still-a-guam-ish and Sky-ko-mish valleys. The tribe known as the Snohomish Indians never extended their territory far above the mouth of the river.

The Puyallups lived along the river of that name and about Commencement bay, while the Nis-qual-lies were most numerous around Olympia and the Stillacoom plains. There were also a number of smaller tribes that have not yet been mentioned who lived for the most part along some portions of the streams or lakes which bear their names. Among them the Duwamish, Samamish, Satsops, Stillacooms, Squaxons, Sumas, Suquamps and Swinomish Indians.

The Makahs around Cape Flattery, as has been stated, were closely related in language with the Indians of Vancouver island and it also appears that the Clallams or the Nus-klai-yums, as they called themselves, were closely connected with them ethnically, but though they show certain affinities for the Nootka dialect there is no doubt but that they belong to the Selish or Flathead stock.

The dialects of the Lummies and Semi-ah-moos have some affinity with the Sanetch dialect of Vancouver island as well as for the Nootka and the Skagit, Samish and Nisqually Indians which strongly approach each other while there are some wide variations among the dialects of some of the intervening tribes.

Of all the languages spoken by the aborigines of the Northwest coast of America the Chinook spoken in various dialects by the tribes around the mouth of the Columbia river is the most intricate. The English vocabulary does not contain words to describe it. To say that it is guttural, clucking, spluttering and the like, is to put it mildly. The Chinook does not appear to have yet discovered the use of tongue and lips in speaking. Like the T'Klinkit of Alaska, their language contains no labials, but the T'Klinkit is music in comparison to it.

CHAPTER VI.

THE CHINOOK LA LANG.

There is danger of falling into error concerning the Chinook jargon, by confusing it with the intricate language of a tribe of that name. On the other hand, people are apt to make the mistake of imputing its invention to a few of the Hudsons Bay company's factors at Astoria. The Chinook jargon was and is yet employed by the white people in their dealings with the natives, as well as by the natives among themselves. It is spoken all over Washington, Oregon, a portion of Idaho and the whole length of Vancouver island. Like other languages formed for convenience it is in all probability a gradual growth. There seems but little doubt that the rudiments of it first existed among the natives themselves and that the trappers and hunters adopted it and improved upon it to facilitate intercourse with the natives. Slowly it was brought to its present state.

When Lewis and Clark reached the coast in 1806, the jargon seems to have already assumed a fixed shape. It was extensively quoted by those explorers. But no English or French words of which it now contains so many, seem to have been added after the expedition sent out by John Jacob Astor reached the coast. The words of the original jargon have been modified to a large extent however. They have been so changed as to eliminate much of the harsh guttural unpronounceable native crackling, thus forming a speech far more suitable to all. In the same manner, some of the English sounds such as "f" and "r," which are so troublesome to the native were either dropped or changed to "p" and "l," and all unnecessary grammatical forms have been eradicated. Even the Chinook jargon is not without its dialects. There are many words used at Victoria that are not used at Seattle or at the mouth of the Columbia. This fact may be accounted for in various ways, but chiefly by the introduction of foreign words. Thus an Indian sees some object that is unfamiliar to him and asks to know the name of it. The trader tells him a name and with him it continues to be the name of the article ever afterward. For example : bread, is always biscuit ; whisky is paih-water, or in some localities, paih-chuck ; a cat is expressed as a puss-puss, an American is a Boston-man, and a Britisher a King-George-man. However, in different localities the things may be named quite differently.

Mr. Gibbs, formerly of the British boundary commission, has stated that the number of Chinook words were about five hundred.   After analyzing the language carefully he classified the words into the various languages from which they originated and came to the following conclusion as to the number of words derived from each :   Chinook and Clatsop, 200 words ; Chinook having analogies with other languages, 21 words ; interjections common to several, 8 words ; Nootka, including dialects, 24 words ; Chehalis, 32, and Nisqually 7 words ; Klikitat and Yakima, 2 words ; Cree, 2 words ; Chippeway, 1 word ; Wasco, 4 words ; Calapooya, 4 words ; by direct onomatopœia, 6 words ; derivation unknown, 18 words ; French, 90 words ; Canadian, 4 words ; English, 67 words.

There are many people who think the Chinook jargon to be the invention of McLaughlin, the Hudsons Bay company's factor at Astoria, but the foregoing facts cited by Mr. Gibbs would seem to indicate that nothing could be further from the truth.   There is no doubt however, that the great fur company assisted it in its development and aided in its spread but even then, American settlers and traders contributed more than the Hudsons Bay company ever did.   It is a remarkable fact that such old Indians as came in contact with the Hudsons Bay company only, could not speak Chinook while the younger class who came in contact with the settlers and traders could all speak it.

It is already on record that Chiefs Sealth and Hettie Kanim belonged to the former class who never learned to speak Chinook.

CHAPTER VII

Jacobs, Big John, William Kitsap and others were among the leading or head men of the tribes on the upper Sound when the whites came. They were given christian names by the early settlers and before their deaths commanded the respect of the whites, who not only learned their simple tongue, but were often regaled with the traditions and history of their tribes. From these men were gleaned the account of the arrival on the upper Sound of the first ship. Before any of these existing Indians were born, so their fathers had imparted to them, during the early part of a "warm sun" (summer time) just after sunset while the Indians were in camp at Beans point, near what are now known as Blakeley rocks, the camp was thrown into great excitement and they ran about the beach uttering exclamations of wonder and astonishment. There upon the bosom of the placid Sound was the first white man's ship with wings outspread. Never had Indian eyes looked upon anything so wonderful. "Uch-i-dah uch-i-dah" wonderful, wonderful. "Ik-tch-o-coke; Ik-tch-o-coke!" what is that, what is that. Then the astonished natives took to the woods, fearing the greatest evil and disaster as they heard for the first time the noise of firing cannon. The more superstitious conceived it a message from the Great Spirit and were filled with the greatest alarm. Old Chief Kitsap was there and the brave old fellow stood his ground and by his demeanor allayed the fears of the more timorous, as well as by pronouncing it a big canoe. It is believed that Kitsap had, on some of his migrations to the lower Sound waters and straits, come in contact with some of the earlier Spanish cruisers. This was the belief of the older Indians at the time of the first white occupation of this country. Both Kitsap and old Chief Sealth had made voyages at that time as far north as what is now Victoria harbor.

The next day following the appearance of the strange visitors, old Kitsap with a few of his sub-chiefs were persuaded to go on board the vessel and were filled with unbounded astonishment at what they saw. It was with an evident relish and much interest that the old Indians above named related through the interpreter Alfred, the story of the visit aboard the first ship, as it was related to them by their fathers and grandsires. Iron, metal goods, knives, forks, chains, firearms and hard bread and other goods were brought out for their inspection. They were offered the hard bread and molasses to eat. The Indians called the latter Ta-gum, which in Chinook means pitch, but after persuasion tasted it and were well pleased and partook of both bread and molasses. Old Kitsap soon made himself at home on board the vessel and the strange white creatures that flitted about her decks were, after the first visit or two, without fear for the sturdy old native. The Indian account, meager as it is, tallies well with Vancouver's record of the same when, for instance, he says it was on the 16th of May, 1792, that he anchored off an island which they named Bainbridge and near a ledge of rocks they called Blakeley rocks.

The Indians' account of Vancouver's movements while anchored off and in view of what is now Seattle harbor or Elliott bay, corresponds with his own. Kitsap piloted Vancouver up the Sound to what is now Olympia. While on this cruise with row-boats they visited the celebrated Old-Man-House at North bay, an Indian rendesvous already mentioned. After an exploring expedition of ten or twelve days up the Sound, old Chief Kitsap as pilot went with Vancouver on a cruise down inside the Whidby island channel to Bellingham bay. Vancouver's ship remained at anchor nearly two moons at Blakeley rocks and the Indians secured of him the first instruments made of iron with which they executed fine carving, after the fashion of the totem posts at the Old-Man-House.

CHAPTER VIII

The history of the Old-Man-House (or as the Indians called it Tsu-Suc-Cub) if fully known would unfold a story as interesting as romance. At this late day its time and surroundings are so shrouded in the mists of the past that but only a glimpse can be had. Its habitats like itself have long years since withered and returned to dust. Probably the best and most authentic account of its history and purpose is the story told by Indian Williams, or as the Indians called him, Sub-Qualth, about 80 or 85 years old at that time, and long since joined to his fathers. Old Williams told his story through an intelligent interpreter also of the Old-Man-House reservation, whose name had been christianized to that of H. S. Alfred.

In the Tsu-Suc-Cub lived eight great chiefs and their people. Space in the big house was allotted to each chief and his people and this was religiously consecrated to them and never encroached upon by others. To old Chief Sealth was given the position of honor; Chief Kitsap came next, Sealth's aged father ranked third, and Tsu-lu-Cub came fourth. These four Sub Qualth remembered and they represented one-half of the Tsu-Suc-Cub. The next four Sub Qualth did not remember but his father, who was a cousin of Chief Sealth had told him their names. There was Bec-kl-lus, Ste-ach-e-cum, Oc-ub, and Lach-e-ma-sub. These were petty chieftains with subordinate tribes and authority and each had a carved totem supposed to properly delineate and perpetuate the deeds of valor of himself and people.

In 1859 there were many of these carved posts remaining and yet standing in fairly good preservation with the big logs still resting on them 16 to 20 feet above the ground. Three of them remained in position in 1870, but during the next fifteen years all were torn down, or falling from decay, were carried off and lost to the historian.

The posts in the front were about 25 feet apart, making the length of the structure over 1,000 feet frontage with the width of the main room fully 60 feet inside. The big corner post was of cedar, as were all of them for that matter, and was of immense size, showing that the tree from which it was cut must have been seven feet through. Clear and distinctly cut on the front of the big totem stood out first and foremost the big Thunderbird in the proportions in which it had fixed itself in the minds of the particular tribe. On the same totem was carved the full sized figure of a man with bow and arrows, representing the old Chief Kitsap, the most noted chief for great strength and prowess on the Sound, save possibly old Sealth.

What a home it must have been. Although the family residing there was large, yet never a resident of Washington lived in a home more spacious. It covered the length and breadth of sandy beach like a king's palace that it was. Three hundred and eighty-four or ninety-four yards, as Wm. Deshaw remem-

ALL THAT'S LEFT OF OLD-MAN-HOUSE

bered, did it stretch away up and down the beach of the narrow Agate passage. Twenty yards or more in breadth it extended back to the edge of the little bluff, where its long timbers rested as on a footstool, and high enough for the tallest Indian brave.

The outlines of the old pile are still readily traceable along the ground although it has been nearly thirty years since the Indians gave it up as a place of abode and took to constructing little huts and lean-tos along the beach and on the gentle slopes above. The attractive relic of the old structure and the one that lends the best idea of the old building's original shape, is one of the log rafters still resting in position on two immense uprights just as it did in the days when the allied tribes hoisted its great weight into the air. It is a cedar log 63 feet long, 12 inches in diameter at the smaller end and probably 23 or 24 inches at the larger end. The uprights, to lend color to the great proportions the old building must have attained, are of immense cedar trees that must have been four feet through. The one nearer the water is 12 feet high and the other fully eight feet. The big timbers were first split asunder and the inside hollowed out and hewn away until a piece probably 10 or 12 inches thick had been left to form the upright. They have been hoisted into position with the convex or bark side turned to face the interior of the house and tamped into the ground until they became solidly set and able to support the great weight that was put on above. Back of the row of uprights that stood at the rear and furthest from the beach, extended another row of stringers or girders to the bank, supporting also a roof, and this greatly enlarged the area of the building. Up and down the beach are numberless posts and foundation blocks of the old house and all in a good state of preservation, as is the single big rafter and two uprights yet in position. These latter are only worn and rotted where they came in contact once with the other or where they enter at the surface of the ground.

An alder bush, a salal bush, and a weed or two have found a foothold in an old wind crack of the rafter and now add to its quaint and picturesque appearance. All else has been torn down or fallen down by the lapse of time and has either floated off with the tide or been burned up in their earthen fires.

Five hundred, six hundred, and as high as seven hundred Indians lived in the big palace here at one time. They lived here long after the white people came among them. The site had been their great village for probably hundreds of years before. Successive chiefs have sat in council here and great war dances and night orgies held through generations of time under the chiefs of the Sealth.

Great banks of crushed and broken and roasted clam shells that whiten the beach and cover the bottom of the sea as with a porcelain lining far out into deep water, attest this better than could have musty scroll or parchment. The entire sea beach extending back onto the high ground is but a bed of decayed clam shells, and even as high up as the Indian farmer's little garden, soil had to be carted in and put upon it, in which the seed germs could take hold and grow. Below it was a bed of lime-like earth, the offal and remains of many thousands of Indian feasts.

Besides the vast amount of crumbled shell mounds there are other and smaller mounds about the site that look as if they might have served the purpose of an elevated fire place. The whole area is overgrown with a thick carpet of short sand grass which even now makes it a most inviting place for campers or picnic parties. Beyond the few things mentioned above there is nothing to remind one now of the iuteresting past hereabouts.

An interesting character still resides, 1895, at the Old-Man-House reservation. He is William Deshaw, whom the tides of time cast upon the beach at Agate point, Kitsap county, 27 years ago.

Deshaw, a rank copper-head to this day, is part of the flotsam and jetsam

WILLIAM DESHAW, THE PIONEER AND INTIMATE FRIEND OF CHIEF SEALTH
From a Life Sketch

that came into the Sound along with the early tide of emigration. He was born in Galveston, Texas, in 1834, and was part of the early drift of Arizona, New Mexico and California. He went into the Sacramento valley a year before the

49ers struck the coast and true to his nature of moving out on the flood tides soon left there and came this way. He has been shot full of arrow holes, and has among numerous other trophies five Indian scalps in his trunk of his own taking. That he ever remained here so long is entirely due to the climate. Let the rains of one long winter on Puget Sound percolate down a man's back and he seldom gets away after that. He takes to it, as it were, like the moss on the roof, and becomes a fixture of the location. And so it was with the old Texan. He drifted in here for a stay of a month or two and he is here yet· He soon got mixed up with the natives, became a squaw man and never after that could he pull himself away. And why should he leave? He had wedded into the royal house of Sealth; wedded a princess, a grand-daughter of the chief of the allied tribes of the Duwamish, Samamish, Squamish, etc., and probably forgot about his old-time habit of drifting. Mrs. Deshaw, nee Princess Mary Sealth, has been dead these many years, and now lies buried in the little reservation churchyard on the hill across the narrow strip of tide water. There are, however, two fine looking girls and some boys left of the union, and in their society the old man is happy and contented. Speaking of the little "God's acre" on the hill near the reservation church reminds us very vividly that within its sacred precincts rests almost all that there is of the races and tribes of Sealth. Eighteen new mounds have been added during the past year. Yet a little while and there will not be a solitary individual left alive to remind those of to-day that such a people ever lived. Father Time has wrought some rapid changes with the allied tribes since the whites came among them. The evil and contaminating influences that have ever followed civilization into the dominion of the simple natives, coupled in this case with their severe and taxing superstitions, have combined to quickly wipe them out of existence.

So quickly have the changes been wrought that whole families have disappeared almost in the night-time. A Siwash with a wife and eight or ten apparently healthy children might wake up to-morrow to find himself a widower without family. Men there are now at the Old-Man-House who have buried their third wife and living with the fourth. Klootchmen were pointed out who have married five different times and only the fifth man living. Chief of Police Jimmy Sealth is the fourth husband of his present wife, who is not over 30 years of age. She lost her first, second and third husbands successively, and with the first one buried seven children. The record of the second and third marriages was not given. Jimmy Sealth, no relation of the old chief, who besides being chief of police, was sheriff, prosecuting attorney, judge and general factotum on the reservation, has been married two or three times and buried two children by his first wife. In one little family plot in the reservation churchyard 23 graves were counted side by side. The dead are not alone buried side by side—they are piled in one on top of another in many cases, although there is a waste of wilderness on every side of the burying ground.

Disease has fallen with a heavy hand upon the allied tribes, but even in the memory of the first white man superstition has done almost as much in the labor of thinning out the population.   Graves there are at the Old-Man-House that have been wet with the blood of human sacrifice within the memory of their great Ta-mahn-a-wis, William Deshaw.   One man there is on the Old-Man-House reservation who has slain 11 children in the practice of their Skal-lal-a-toot, or hoodooism, and whose blood saturated the tomb of their hy-as-tyees.

Such in a few words is the rather sympathetic story of a people who here-abouts were the first in the land.   A people whose Ta-mahn-a-wis men, or great medicine men, foretold the coming of the white people days and days before the Indians themselves saw the ships of Vancouver sailing, sailing from out the heavy cloud banks and high up in the air, for from such a source did the three ships appear to the simple natives as told now in some of their traditions.   The Old-Man-House, or Port Madison Indian reservation lies about 15 miles northwest of Seattle and not far from the Port Madison mills, one of the big lumber camps of Puget Sound, now idle and almost tenantless, a result as much probably of extensive litigation as anything else.   It is a mill town owned exclusively by the mill company, which furnishes all the employment of the place to its 300 or 400 inhabitants when the mill is busy.   Now that there is nothing to do in the mill there is no occasion for remaining there and the mill men with their families have moved elsewhere and the rows of pretty whitewashed cottages are empty and voiceless.

The mill property is situated in a pretty little bight of the Sound, once a favorite nook of the Indians, hid away from view until one is right upon it.   It is located nearly at the northernmost end of Bainbridge island, and the mill town at one time besides supporting a considerable mill population, was the county seat of Kitsap county.   But during a few years past, however, the most officious and omnipresent individual over there was the court's officer, who held the keys to the mill and looked after the property for the court pending final adjudication of the case on behalf of all litigants.

The Indian reservation lies about three miles distant from the mill and separated from it by Agate passage, a narrow thread of water 900 feet across at half tide.

The way over to the reservation is nothing more than a narrow trail hewn out of the woods a few feet up from the beach, and was apparently first cut by the men who strung the old Puget Sound telegraph and cable company's wire to the lower Sound.

At the extreme limit of Bainbridge island is Agate point and directly across,

GRAND POTLATCH—OLD-MAN-HOUSE.

the reservation. On the point is the old trading store of William Deshaw, first started in the early sixties, and has been a trading store ever since. Deshaw has been left in undisturbed possession ever since and there he is to-day, probably his only accumulation being his now motherless but happy family of half-breed boys and girls. Every nook and corner hereabouts appears remindful of the musty past, everything is interesting to look upon or ruminate over. Deshaw's old trading store is a museum of antiquities, and its restless, gray-haired and slippered proprietor is the one living specimen and most interesting of all there is on exhibition. Sixty years old, yet he is apparently as full of vitality as he ever was. There is just as much fire in his small gray eyes and as much of a spring in the step as there was when he was taking the scalp-locks of the bloodthirsty Comanche and Apaches.

The old gentleman hearing our approach one Wednesday morning came shambling out onto his front porch and was soon in the midst of an interesting talk on the Indians with whom for so long he has been associated. Although the better part of his life he has spent among the tribes that first held possession of the wooded shores of the Sound here, he is by no means an Indian lover, especially of the renegade set which now has possession of Old-Man-House village. He has without doubt during the last 25 years talked twice as much Chinook and pure Siwash as English yet he uses the strongest expletives of the English tongue in speaking of his present Indian neighbors. "Lo, the poor Indian," finds no sympathy in his breast. He thinks it a great pity that 14,800 acres of land should be kept exclusively for a few shiftless and unworthy Indians to live upon it to the exclusion of the white people, and so it appears. They have had these lands for generations yet there is just the narrowest border of clearing along the waters that bears any resemblance to cultivation, and that for the most part is due to the labor of a few white men rather than to the Indians.

"They never would work," says Deshaw, "and never will. Kindness is wasted upon them ; every kind act done them is returned with an injury."

Probably the otherwise kind-hearted old man would not talk so but for the fact that the old Indians, those who gave allegiance to old Chief Sealth, have all been crowded out and either dead or driven away and become lost in other tribes by renegade Indians. These last are "cultus" people, who have been run out of and off other reservations and becoming wanderers and veritable Indian tramps have at last found a stopping place at Old-Man-House.

Deshaw says there are about 60 inhabitants on the reservation, big, little, old, young and indifferent, but the agent would probably give a larger number. Of these, he counts but six that are truly men of the allied tribes, once ruled by old Chief Sealth. These men are Big John, now chief, Charley Shafton, Charley Uk-a-ton, Charley Ke-ok-uk, one of the two honest Indians on the reservation, according to Deshaw, George Thle-wah and Jacob Huston, one of the old-time Indians, but a slave. None of these are of the family or descendants of the old chief though the families of Big John and Jacob have always been considered among the nobility of the allied tribes. Not even all the six Indians mentioned are good Indians, for Deshaw reckons but five on the reservation who care for a home or make any effort toward providing for their necessities in the way the white men have taught them. They prefer to keep to their old customs and superstitions; would rather troll for salmon and send their klootchmen to dig for clams than plant potatoes or milk a cow. Two or three years without the watchful care of the government and the very few whites who take interest enough to look after them, and they would drift back into a barbarism as deep as that of 50 years ago. The government pays a man to reside upon the reservation in the capacity of Indian farmer to see to it that the men with families and homes do something toward raising gardens and gather the fruit that ripens in the little orchards. The Indian agent proper does not reside there but anon visits the spot in his official capacity. That personage lives at Tulalip, Lummi, Old-Man-House reservation, Muk-il-shoot and one other. The present Indian farmer, J. Y. Roe, and his wife, have been upon the reservation a little over a year and are full of sympathy for the wards they watch over. They have done much to improve the situation on the reservation and give up all their time and a portion of the small pittance they receive, $50 a month, to do the work. Among the improvements in the village on the reservation the farmer has accomplished is the building of a new court house or town hall and "skookum" house, and a number of other things in the way of improvements to the small gardens and orchards.

The reservation forms a large body of land which ends in a beautiful peninsula between Squim bay and the narrows. The site of the reservation village which is also the site of the famous Old-Man-House, fronts the water on the south in a gentle slope, covered with half grown evergreens and the narrowest border of cleared lands set to orchards, flower gardens and vegetables. The most conspicuous figure of the village is the Catholic church, a perfect little model in its way, and as white and gleaming in the sun as a snowy peak. It will bear the utmost scrutiny for it is just the same in or out, far or near. By far the most interesting thing to be found there at this day is the relic of the Old-Man-House, which can just be made out from the porch of the old trading store on the opposite side of the bay. It is down close to the water's edge and about midway in the little clearing. But how can one be expected to glean anything from its past and old associations without the presence of the big Tah-mahn-a-wis man along. So Mr. Deshaw shambled away after his big, rusty key, locks up his store and goes off for a whole day with us, perfectly unconcerned as to the propriety of good business methods.

At the waters's edge on the reservation side of the narrows lives the Indian farmer, a sub-agent, and his spouse, a very easy-going, plodding, pleasant natured old couple. Old-Man-House is usually as serene and quiet as a Sabbath day, in fact every day is a Sunday in this respect.

There is a school, but no business, no nothing but what would prove to a white person a monotonous and unbearable existence. There is one irregular and vagrant looking street connecting with a little beaten trail that leads to the cemetery on the hill. Here is the populous part of the village. We lead the way into the inclosure and through the windings between the thickly made mounds, a large portion of which have a little emblem of the crucifixion raised above them. The old Texan with us has known, in their day, most of the Indians who are sleeping the last quiet sleep here and hesitates not to indicate who were the cultus and who were the good Indians. "That fellow," he would say, "was as big a rascal as ever lived," or of another, "he was a good Indian and a hard worker." Directly he leads the way up near the north side of the inclosure where a large marble monument marks the resting place of some big tyee. There are a dozen small mounds in the same little plot and ranged on either side of it, but the only inscription is on the big monument and it reads :

SEATTLE

Chief of the Suquamps and allied tribes

Died June 7, 1866

The firm friend of the whites, and for him

the city of Seattle was named by

its founders

On the reverse is inscribed the following :

Baptismal name, Noah Sealth.   Age probably

80 years.

That is the only bit of history there is about or on the monument. The little plot is not enclosed, and the weeds have full possession. The dozen or more graves in the same plot are of the family of the old chief, but the Texan fails now to call them by name. He however takes exception to the inscription as being incorrect, and in part superfluous. He objects to the name Sealth or Seattle, but says the Indian pronunciation was as near Se-at-tlee as the English language can reproduce it. The word Sealth, says Deshaw, was the translation of the old settlers who lived on Elliott bay. The old chief himself spoke the name for him a thousand times or more as given above, as did the people of the Old-Man-House. The Indians never knew the old chief by the name of Noah, that word being used probably but once, and that at the time of his baptism into the Catholic faith.

There are graves of other old-time chiefs in the little churchyard, the most

conspicuous one being that of Alex. George, whose little monument is sur-
rounded by twenty-two other graves, all enclosed in a neat white-washed picket
fence. They are all of the immediate family of the dead chieftain.

On the way back to the village we stop and inspect the garden and orchard
of the boss gardener of the Indians, John Kettle. Besides himself and wife, he
has about a score of dogs of every hair and color, which set up a perfect pandemonium as we approach. Kettle is one of the old slaves, a Clayoquot sound,
or West coast Indian, who was sold to a chief of the allied tribes when a boy
by some other tribe who had captured him and brought him into the Sound
country. Kettle seemed pleased at the interest shown his garden and orchard
and said he had 160 acres of fine land, and some day would be a rich Indian.

Kettle when brought into the allied tribes' camp could not speak a word of

THE OLD-MAN-HOUSE VILLAGE AS IT APPEARS TO-DAY

their language nor could they understand him. He was almost starved. The
old chief who bought him was with the family eating from a big kettle of
roasted or boiled clams. When Siwash and Chinook failed, the old chief
motioned to his slave to eat clams. John didn't wait for a second bidding, and
soon finished the kettle of clams. Then another kettle filled with the bivalves
was prepared for him. John had heard the Indians speak the word kettle several times when dipping into the pot and he took the word to mean clams. So
John began to call out as best he could, "kettle, kettle." "Umph," cried the
old chief in Siwash, "he wants more clams. I have it, that will be his name,
John Kettle," and from that day to this the new slave was called John Kettle.
The fellow is not over 35 years old, but his wife, who has been married five
or six times and had a cultus husband every time, and who has been beaten all

through her life, looks as if she might be John Kettle's grandmother instead of his spouse.

The first " Boston " house built on the reservation is still standing and occupied by one of the chief men of the village. It was built entirely at the expense of William Deshaw as his first free offering towards a reform in the mode of life of the Old-Man-House Indians. This was a reform very much desired by the government at that time, but towards the accomplishment of which it did very little according to Mr. Deshaw.

The Old-Man-House agency was, according to this authority, very much of a sinecure to the early agents, a half dozen of whom he thinks, probably never set foot on the agency. Deshaw for several years acted as a sub-agent for these appointees and virtually had the say in everything at Old-Man-House or that concerned the allied tribes. He got to be such a trusted lieutenant that he would be intrusted with large sums of money to spend for the Indians and at one time had $ 18.000 which the government gave him and with which he bought supplies in Portland. This was during the incumbency of the late George D. Hill of Seattle as Indian agent. Hillory Butler of Seattle was another agent for whom Mr. Deshaw looked after things at Old-Man-House.

The first great duty with which the government charged Mr. Deshaw was the breaking up of the Old-Man-House and the isolation of the 600 or 800 Indians in separate households with the idea of inculcating civilized ideas of living. It was a hard task and one fraught with many disappointments before it was accomplished. The Indians were a curious lot. To-day they were your friends ; to-morrow they were ready to plug you full of lead from an old Hudsons bay company's musket. Finally he got one or two to make the first attempts at separate residence and by degrees got them all out of the building and ruined it from further inhabitancy. But in almost every instance the Indians wanted the work all done by the sub-agent and refused to lend a hand themselves.

Old Chief Sealth was a great power at Old-Man-House and lived for several years after Mr. Deshaw went among them. He became very friendly with the sub-agent and accepted his advice in everything and tried to make his people live up to the orders of the great father at Washington City. According to Deshaw, the old chief was greatly reverenced and to as great degree feared by the Indians. Sealth gave all the assistance in his power to Deshaw in an effort to break up the heathenish practices of the Ta-mahn-a-wis men and destroy the superstition of their scal-al-a-toots, but these evils were never eradicated and to this day, but for the ridicule cast upon them by the whites, they would still practice them openly.

The habit of burying their dead in trees and elevated places was in vogue long after Deshaw went among them, but was never done openly or with the consent of the old chief. Even the baneful practice of slaying the dead chief's horse or dog and his slaves on the grave was religiously carried out for several years after Deshaw's appearance whenever the Indians could do it with safety. Deshaw tells of one prominent Indian now living on the reservation, Huston, who was a slave at that time and who was with his klootchman and his little daughter doomed to suffer death on the grave of their master, Chief Ska-ga-ti-quis. Huston got wind of what the Indians were about to attempt and, with his klootchman and 12-year-old girl, slipped away in a canoe to the other side of the narrows and took refuge in Deshaw's trading store. Seventeen big and brawny bucks with Hudsons bay company muskets followed the refugees over and stormed the store. They rushed in clamorous and gesticulating and swinging their guns, and demanded their prisoners, saying they were going to kill them over Ska-ga-ti-quis' grave. The prisoners were hid away in a little side building. Deshaw began parleying with the blood-thirsty fellows and directly several of them carelessly lay their guns on the counter. Deshaw, without attracting attention, moved up close to them and quickly pulled the guns over and allowed them to fall on the floor back of the counter. Almost at the same time old Chief Sealth, who had heard of the trouble at the store, quickly got into a canoe, paddled across and went rushing into the store. The old chief possessed a powerful voice and herculean strength.

"Whoo, whoo, do I hear ; what do I hear," he cried several times upon his entry, but the Indians began falling back and said never a word. Then the old chief's little grand-daughter, one of Mr. Deshaw's daughters, yet living, went up to the old gray head and in her Indian and childish way said, "Grand-pa, they are going to kill the Hustons over Ska-ga-ti-quis' grave."

Then, "whoo, whoo," puffed the old chief, and grabbing up a musket, prepared to slay every Indian in sight, but the Indians knew the old fellow's temper too well and shot out of the doorway in a twinkling, and went pell-mell into the water and scrambled into their canoes. The old chief rushing after them grabbed up a big cedar rail, after dropping the gun (it was entirely too light for him), and tried to reach them with that, but they got away and across back to the village. The old chief kept right after them, and once on his own side called the whole village together and made the people a speech.

He could be heard distinctly on the opposite side of the channel haranguing them on the evil of killing their slaves.

"Mr. Deshaw, the big white medicine, did not want it done, Governor Stevens did not want it, Colonel Simmons did not want it, and the great chief at Washington City did not want it, and it must stop." Such was the speech, as now remembered and translated by one of those most interested in the occurrence. The speech seemed to have a good effect, at least for the time. Guards were placed over the Hustons, and they remained out of sight for a week or more, and no attempt was again made to take and kill them in so barbarous a way. Until quite recently several very aged Siwash resided at the Old-Man-House reservation. There was Jacob, aged about 75 years, a grandson of the old Chief Kitsap ; old man Williams, aged about 85 ; William Kitsap, grandson of old Chief Kitsap, and H. S. Alfred, both educated Indians. Old William's daughter married a Kitsap county pioneer who as the years went by grew rich and prominent and his half-breed progeny promise to become honorary and intelligent members of society.

When old Williams was a boy his people were very numerous and happy, and dwelt on the borders of the salt water from Vashon island to Port Town-send. On the beach in front of Tsu-Suc-Cub, were drawn up at all times hundreds of canoes, so many that all the beach was covered with them. Many thousands of Indians gathered and lived in the big Tsu-Suc-Cub, and the country round about it. There were so many that chiefs Sealth and Kitsap were very big Indians, and were not afraid of any warlike tribes. Sealth the first, and Chief Kitsap once headed an expedition against the Cape Flattery and Victoria Indians, but this was at so early a date that William himself was too young to take part. His father was a brave and helped fight the enemy. At the head of great numbers of war canoes they raided the villages of the tribes on both sides of the straits, and at Victoria harbor a great battle was fought. The older Chief Sealth, or as he is sometimes spoken of, Sealth the First, it was said could drive an arrow through the side of the biggest canoe, and his strength was most wonderful. This expedition was an epoch in the. Indian history of the Puget Sound natives. It was successful and the raids that had annually been made by the tribes from the north on the southern Indians of the Sound ceased, and it was due to the bravery of the two chiefs Sealth First and Second, that it was so. To the latter was due the glory of putting a stop to the invasions of Puget Sound Indians by the tribes east of the mountains. Sealth the Second, he for whom the city of Seattle was named, exercised late in his life so powerful an influence over near-by tribes that he was able to consolidate six tribes into one, which took the name of Duwamish or the allied tribes. He was an orator ; an arbitrator rather than a great war-rior, and with the exception perhaps of a great campaign to head off the invading Indians from east of the mountains which he executed at one time most successfully, never was engaged in any great battle. Not only was that affair well planned, but it proved a great and decisive battle. No whites were living on Puget Sound at the time. There are no recorded facts regarding it. It was told by the father to the son, and was one of the cherished memories which the whites first heard when they arrived.

Old Williams was asked who did the carving on the totems and why no work of the kind had been done since the whites came among them. The old fellow said that long ago there were many skilled carvers of totems and fine canoe builders and their implements were made from flints, agates and elk horn, fashioned into the shape of rude hatchets and knives. Many, many years before, while the old Indian was but a little boy, one of the chiefs of that day secured a piece of iron or steel from a Spanish trader, and for years after this piece of iron was turned to good account by the canoe builders in the tribes in making their canoes. Before the year 1800, or about that time, as arrived at by computing the time given in his aboriginal way by old William, only horn and agate hatchets and shell instruments were used in the work of totem carving or canoe building. These rude instruments were fastened on to rude handles wound around and bound around, and were deftly handled in carving and fashioning the softer woods as alder and maple into totems, canoes or bows and arrows.

Then came Vancouver, and from him old Kitsap procured a good supply of knives and iron which for fifty years after were used and in the keeping of the tribesmen, replacing the older instruments of their ancestors.

CHAPTER IX

In the days and generations past, when the Indians were the only people who occupied the shores of Puget Sound, the Twana tribe, now the Skokomish, lived in the broad strip of territory bordering on the west side of Hood's canal and extending back to the top of the Olympic mountains and reaching from the Skokomish river on the south to Quilcene, near Port Townsend, on the north. They had for neighbors on the south and east the Squaxon tribe, while near them on the north and northwest were the Clallams and Ma-kahs. On the west were the Quillayutes and Quiniaults, but as the high mountains intervened there was not much intercourse in that direction, either in peace or war. The Twanas apparently much preferred peace to war and happiness on their own hunting and fishing grounds to pillage and robbery, for there are no old-time battle grounds pointed out now as having been once the scene of great carnage among them. However, they were Indians and as remarkable for their extreme and foolish superstitions and baneful practices as any on the Sound.

They possessed a fine country, especially the beautiful valley of the Skoko-mish river, which today is one of the prettiest places in the state. When the government made a treaty with these Indians and took most of their land away from them it left them the best section of all their territory for a perma-nent home. That was the ground at the mouth of the river on the north bank. Here resides the remnant of the Twanas, which, however, is composed of the blood of three former tribes, the Skokomish proper, Quilcenes and Duhl-ay-lips, the head Indian agent for whom is stationed at the beautiful agency of Tulalip on the east side of the Sound.

There are about 200 of these mongrel Indians now living on the reservation of 5,997 acres at the mouth of the river. Twenty years ago there were but about 250 of them, so that the decrease in population has been comparatively very small. In 1880 a census taken that year showed 237 Indians. In 1890, ten years from that time, there had been 100 deaths on the reservation, but the increase in population from birth alone was such that the real decrease was not more than fifteen persons. There is little if any increase to the population from people settling there from other tribes. This showing is better than that of any Indian tribe on the Sound, and is undoubtedly due to the isolation on the west side of the canal and removal from the contaminating influence of worthless white people. One beneficial effect of late years, really for the past thirty or forty years, has been the example of a few good farmers who settled in the fine valley of the Skokomish. Then to, they have always been blessed with good Indian agents, which cannot be said to have been always the case at many other reservations. The Indians generally nowadays work well and want to work and make good lumbermen in the logging camps, earning almost as much as the white men when the camps are going.

The Indian lands are patented to him but are owned in severalty and there are many creditable places at Skokomish. There is assigned to a single Indian from 80 to 170 acres according to whether the land may be all valley or partially hills. No matter how much or how little land an Indian may possess, he seldom, if ever, gets beyond the point of a small truck farmer. If he happens to get under cultivation an area that would by a stretch of the imagination take the name of a field, he is most sure to let out the land to a white farmer on an annual cash basis. There are a few such cultivated fields at Skokomish. A farmer, whether Indian or white, whose insane desire for gambling will lead him to spend a whole night out in the woods chanting the monotonous song of the "sing-gamble" pot-latch, at harvest time is not expected to prove a howling success as a granger.

In another generation if there are any Twana Indians left they will probably rate as first-class farmers, for the government is progressing very well in the matter of training them. The children attend school ten months in the year, have good instructors chosen from the whites, and the boys have over them a special instructor whose duty it is to see that they work half of every week-day, with a view of acquiring methodical and industrious habits. This is abhorrent to the tender Indian mind, but as the entire education of the Twana youth is one of the charity undertakings of the government and does not cost the old folks a cent, they seem to like it and force their youngsters to attend. The maintenance of the schools is kept up by yearly appropriations and could be cut off any time if the government cared to do so. In that case the little Twana might be permitted to spring up as unconscious of the future as the weeds that infest the door-yard and garden patch of every Indian domicile. However, among the Twanas there is already a fair standard of rudimentary education acquired, for every Indian below 30 years of age can read and write English, and all under 40 can talk the language. The true specimens of the savage ancestors are the old men and women yet living, who cannot, rather will not, admit to any knowledge of the English.

The Indian here is an obdurate, slow-moving being. He will begin a thing but complete it in a year, or ten years, or never, just as the notion takes him. At this time the residents have in mind the construction of a new church. They have gone so far in the undertaking as to have secured the lumber and floated it from the mill up the river and piled it upon the bank of the stream on the reservation.

"We got it long time ago," said one fellow, "to build a new church, but don't know whether we will ever build it or not."

The vicinity of the old lumber pile now seems to be a favorite rendesvous for the inveterate "sing-gamble" players, for they ride there from all directions at night time. They light camp fires and, forming a large circle around it, go through their uncanny practices until the cocks crow for morning.

All the male population of the reservation over age are voters under the constitution of the United States. They cast their first vote at the election for delegates to the state constitutional convention after the passage by Congress of the enabling act. The reservation has been set off in a precinct by itself, and by this the Indians elect their own justices of the peace and petty officers without the interference of the whites and without having anything to do themselves with the election of officers to govern the white people.

In the very nature of things the Chinook and mother tongues will, in a few years more, be unknown on the reservation. So rapidly is this coming about that at this time half the conversation of the reservation is carried on in English, even when all engaged in it are Indians. At their sing-gamble and other Indian ceremonies English is as much spoken as their own tongue.

Superstition will only die out of the Indian mind when the last of the race is dead and gone. On the banks of the lovely Skokomish it would seem that superstition could have no abiding place. Yet it is there today as it probably has been in all the past thousands of years. The beneficent influence of the white man's religion has superceded it in its outer and practical application, but it is only a few years ago when the efficacy of the red and black "ta-mahn-a-wis" was thought to be greater than all the religions of the pale faces in the world.

There were four kinds of ta-mahn-a-wis, sometimes spelled ta-mahn-o-us, or spirit practices in vogue among the Twanas as there were among the great family of Selish Indians in Washington, which included most all, but not all, the tribes from the Spokane river to Cape Flattery, all understanding in part a common language. The Cape Indians and Yakimas are two of the exceptions to the above, according to some of the best informed men on the subject. The word ta-mahn-a-wis may be and was used in the sense of a noun, an adjective or a verb. As a noun it means any kind of a spirit in the spirit world from the Sahg-ha-lie Tyee, or supreme being—sahg-ha-lie meaning greatest, highest, above—to the klail ta-mahn-a-wis, or devil, literally, black spirit.

As an adjective a ta-mahn-a-wis stick, stone, person, etc., is a thing or individual with a ta-mahn-a-wis or spirit either of good or evil in it. As a verb it is used in the sense of invoking the aid of spirits, as " mah-mok ta-mahn-a-wis."

The four kinds of ta-mahn-a-wis of the Indians of the Twana tribe at least are : The " ta-mahn-a-wis over the sick," the incantations of the medicine men ; the " red ta-mahn-a-wis," the " black ta-mahn-a-wis," and the " spirit land ta-mahn-a-wis."

The sick ta-mahn-a-wis was only practiced for the healing of the sick, and was often a severe and taxing ordeal for the patient if he were really sick. This ceremony was always conducted by the ta-mahn-a-wis men assisted by the friends and relatives of the sick in an effort to drive out the spirit of one that was supposed to have taken possession of the body of the sick.

The red ta-mahn-a-wis was a winter pastime and was a common arrangement, a proceeding, so far as its being a part of a religious belief, a kind of a camp-meeting. The red, or pill ta-mahn-a-wis, was an assembling together, an invocation, in short, of the spirits for a good season the following summer. It generally lasted three or four days and consisted of singing, dancing, the beating of tom-toms, drums and the decoration of the face and limbs and body invariably with streaks and spots of red paint. From this it was given the name of the red ta-mahn-a-wis, pill meaning red.

The black, or klail ta-mahn-a-wis, was without doubt the one great religion of all religious practices among them. It was a secret society to a very large extent, and none but the initiated were ever permitted to have anything to do with it. It was a very severe initiation that candidates had to undergo to get acquainted with it, and little was ever learned of its mysteries by the whites. It was practiced at Skokomish as late as 1876, but after that time it was never seen. At that time it was given out by the participants that it was to be dead after that. It is said that it is still slightly followed by the Clallam Indians to this day. No doubt but that among the residents of the Skokomish reservation there are many Indians who were initiated into its dreadful mysteries, but their number is probably too few to revive it. Both men and women were initiated into the practice and mysteries of the black ta-mahn-a-wis. The significance of this ceremony, from the secretiveness of the Indians, was never clearly learned by the old residents, who had most to do with the Indians, and it probably will never be understood, at least as it was believed in by the various tribes.

In the practice of it, however, the Indians invariably painted themselves very hideously with black paint, daubing and streaking the face and limbs, and while going through the ceremony of initiation were without clothing. Masks made in rude imitation of the wolf head were used, and these were called shway-at-sho-sin. The mask was adopted by the Twanas from the Clallam tribe, as was the name and hence the word is the same in both languages. The Twanas seem to have imported their masks from the Clallam country in most part, very few of their own make having ever been found, and these of a less degree of artistic appearance. To a certain extent the ceremony of the black ta-mahn-a-wis was a public one and many of the old-timers have witnessed that portion of it. The more important and probably much more severe part was the private ceremony confined to the initiated. The public ceremony was a long drawn out affair of dancing, singing, beating of drums and tom-toms, rattles, etc. During the progress of the affair the candidates for whose special benefit the ta-mahn-a-wis was given, were stripped and painted and put through all manner of gyrations and exercises, the while wearing the wolf mask, that in the least resemble the antics of the animals they were trying to imitate. While this was going on the candidates were tied about the middle with a long rope, the loose end of which was held by other Indians in order to keep the candidate from running away or from doing harm to any spectator, for he was supposed to do just like a ferocious and enraged wolf in all things. The other exercises which are supposed to put on the finishing touches to the great event, were always carried on in secret rooms made of their blankets or tents and were never permitted to be witnessed.

The practice of the spirit land ta-mahn-a-wis was associated with or founded on a very pretty myth believed in by the old Twanas to the effect that a year or two perhaps before an Indian died he or she lost his or her spirit. Spirits from other places, always from below, would visit the Indian and, quite unaware to the person would take and carry off the spirit and sail with it to their abiding place, there to hold it in captivity unless released by spirits from this life. Whenever an Indian lost his spirit in this way there would always be a little left him which would be sufficient to last him until he died, by which time every particle of it was absorbed, vanished, gone. To elaborate the fanciful theory, there were always living Indians who professed to be able to go to the spirit land, down below, and see what was going on and recognize spirits taken from Indians of his own tribe and village. These trips may be made to the spirit regions at the will of the Indians, sometimes when off in the hills hunting, or when out on the salt water chasing the whale or the seal. After a journey of such a character the Indian's word was never doubted by his tribe's people, when he on returning informed them that he had been on a journey below and had seen the captured spirits of this or that relative or friend. The next question was as to the recovery of the spirit, and there were always willing hands ready to assist.

There was always great ceremony, great care and at times extreme caution to be maintained in this undertaking. The Indians had to make the journey down below, cross their death river, their river Styx, and perform various other and wonderful feats, the entire ceremony lasting three or four days.

The first ceremony, accompanied by a great beating of drums, of rattles, tom-toms, dancing, singing, chanting and yelling, is that of breaking the ground to effect an entrance below. This was done by digging a little hole in the dirt floor of the house where the ceremony was taking place. This accomplished, other mythical performances were gone through with, the more important one being "cooning" across the Styx river in a long procession, where the greatest caution was observed, for the warrior who should fall off while going over was doomed to die before long. A bridge was constructed of boards in the house by having two of the boards resting obliquely against the ends of a third board, which is elevated to near the roof of the building. The army on the chase for the lost spirit "cooned it" across this improvised bridge, and were then over the river Styx into spirit land. They searched for and with great noise and hubbub found the departed spirit, took possession of it amidst a great and imaginary battle, and returned to the land of the living. They would tear about the room during this performance, rant and roar, run out of and around the house, tear the roof off in their frenzy, which was truly a genuine article, and then, after having reached the limit of their strength and exertion, would find the spirit, sometimes in the form of a rag doll or some other object just as ridiculous, and carry it in triumph to the Indian who had lost his spirit. This individual, so fortunate in recovering his spirit, and therefore a new lease of life, is overjoyed at the thought and laughs and cries alternately, and concluded the performance by a great manifestation of joy in every conceivable style.

At this ceremony the Indians had an idol which exercised a great power, in their overwrought imaginations, in the success of the undertaking. This idol was a very sacred being, and was always kept hid away in the mountains and never brought out only on such ceremonies. It was never given up to the whites, and there is probably not now one of these strange things to be found anywhere. The only one known to have been seen among the Twana tribe was about four feet long, of very rude carving, in imitation of a person without arms or feet. In place of feet the idol ended in a stick, so made that it could be fastened firmly in the ground. It was raised in the center of the room, and around it the weird and uncanny ceremony progressed. This idol the Indians named Sh-but-ta-dahk, but just what its peculiar properties were probably is not known.

Several of the more intelligent and younger men on the reservation were talked to about this idol or totem, but they did not know anything about its history or supposed properties. One of the men said that about three years ago, while going through the woods about three miles back of the reservation, he came across a cache where there were two of these idols hid away. They were time-worn and considerably decayed, and, as he stated, had "been there long, long time." He placed them under an old tree, but never returned to get them. They had men's faces carved upon them, and were undoubtedly genuine Sh-but-ta-dahks.

There is another one about four or five feet long in the possession of a resident of Lake Cushman, which was found in the woods about ten or twelve miles back of the present reservation. Many, probably all, of the Indians of today on the reservation have faith in the Sh-but-ta-dahk and the ceremony of the spiritland, ta-mahn-a-wis. One, in telling about it, said that not many years ago a spirit-land ta-mahn-a-wis was held, when one of the Indians fell while crossing the death river, and that a short time after he died, hence they knew that the spirit-land ta-mahn-a-wis was true.

The theory of the medicine ta-mahn-a-wis is that when a person is sick some evil spirit has taken possession of the body, sometimes more than one evil spirit, and of different kinds. It may be that of a bird or beast, a bear, a panther, wolf, a bluejay or a weasel, or anything else having hair or feather or scale. It was always the duty of the ta-mahn-a-wis doctors to find out what kind of a spirit had entered the body, and then by incantation and ceremony to drive it out. Some dry board or rail or piece of wood was secured by the friends of the patient and placed conveniently near, and on this they would beat with sticks to make as much noise as possible, also bringing into their aid the drum and tom-toms or rattles. The medicine man would take a bowl of water by the side of the patient, who had been stretched out on a mat on the ground, and begin his examinations. He would chant in a monotonous way and perform various mysterious things about and over the sick person. Sometimes he would take hold of an arm or a leg and lift apparently with all his strength without so much as moving the member in the least. When the din and hubbub would be sufficiently distracting the medicine man generally discovered what kind of a spirit had taken possession, and was able to get hold of it. Often he would raise that part of the person in which the spirit had secured a place of lodgment, and would douse it in the bowl of water and drown it. At other times he would draw it out of the body by inhaling it in his own lungs, and would then go to the door and give a great puff and blow the evil spirit far across the mountains or water.

If, under such a course, the patient did not get well at once, there was, of course, other evil spirits in the body which must be gotten rid of, and the process would be repeated with minor variations. By and by the patient would either get well naturally or die, which ended the matter. In either case, the potent power of the doctor was never questioned. The Indians believed that while the body was in possession of the evil spirit, the Indian's spirit may take its flight to some distant place temporarily. It was part of the duty of the medicine man to locate and bring the absent spirit back. This he did by other and mystical processes equally as absurd to civilized minds. In one account, which was written out by an educated brother of a sick boy at the Skokomish reservation, the departed spirit of the patient was discoved 15 miles distant at what the Indians called Du-hub-hub-ai, now called by the whites Humi-humi. The evil spirit always took on very curious shapes when drawn on paper by the Indians for the edification of the whites. They usually represented very vaguely images of fish, jelly-fish, imaginary beasts, etc.

That the Indians of the Skokomish tribe once engaged in war is evidenced by the existence of implements of battle now preserved on the reservation. Of their war clubs there is one about twelve inches long, which weighs three and a half pounds. It is a big wedge shaped affair, rounded, and recedes sharply to a blunt point. There is a hole drilled in the handle end by which it could be suspended from the warrior's waist with buckskin thongs. This weapon was made, without doubt, by the Skokomish or Twana tribe.

Another war implement and one much more formidable, is a long copper club, two feet long, much in appearance like a broad sword. This club also has a hole in the heavier end, from which to suspend it to the waist. Both weapons have rude imitations of the Thunderbird on their heavier ends, and go to show how thoroughly the Thunderbird myth was believed in and how it pervaded every act and thought of Indian life.

Before the white people came into the country the Indians had to depend on their own ingenuity for all kinds of implements. Many of these are yet preserved by the Indians themselves, as well as by the whites. The Indians are careless, however, and as long as they can get an easy living, don't seem to care much what becomes of their old tools. They have yet a few of the old war clubs, among them, ta-mahn-a-wis rattles, made out of deer hoofs, bear and beaver teeth, etc. They have a few of the old style bows and arrows, hunting bows, with quivers of arrows to be used in the chase or in war. The latter are of a superior workmanship, and must have occupied lots of extra time in their manufacture. They have few of the old style dress garments, but have not yet lost the art of manufacture, as they will for money set about and make very interesting dresses and coats out of the cedar bark, or from the cat-tail reeds that grow in the swamps or marsh lands. There is yet preserved several specimens of the dress of the nobility, made from the hair of the mountain goat, though it is not unlikely that these latter were secured in barter from the tribes occupying land on the east side of Puget Sound, as the mountain goat is not known to have flourished between Puget Sound and the Pacific ocean.

The Twanas' and perhaps many of the other Indian tribes' superstition as to the origin of the sun and moon is of more than passing interest. A very long while ago there lived an aged Indian woman who had a son. He must have been a bright, uncommon lad, for he was not only stolen from home, but grew up into a young man possessing wonderful powers. The boy was stolen from the care of his grandmother and carried away to distant parts, beyond the mountains, where if anyone tried to follow, the mountains would come together and crush the life out of them. When the boy's mother learned he had been stolen she was greatly grieved, and declared she would find her another son, and so she did. He grew apace and became also a bright promising lad. By and by, as the days passed away, the first son found his way back through the treacherous mountains and surprised his mother when he put in an appearance at home once more. He does not seem to have been pleased at the prospect of finding his place at home taken by a brother, and he at once declared he would change the brother into the moon, and let him rule the world by night, while he himself would be changed into the sun and govern things by day. This shows that the family to which this ambitious young man belonged was a great family, and probably governed the world before that time in darkness.

The young man kept his word and wrought the marvelous changes, and it must have occasioned great surprise next morning when the people got up and found all the land aglow with light and beauty. But as the sun got up higher, the people doubtless wished for their darkness back again, for it got awfully hot. The brother—as the sun—in his great wrath burned A GUARDIAN SPIRIT TOTEM so fiercely that the heat dried up all the rivers of the country and killed off all the fishes, and the people of the land sweltered and died in the suffocating heat that pervaded everything.

The brother saw that things could not last long in this way, and he decided on a change. So he changed things about, made his weaker and younger brother into the sun and himself into the moon, and this worked better. Ever since that day there has always been "a man in the moon," and a boy in the sun, but the light of the latter is too strong for the boy's face to be seen.

The Skal-lal-a-toot was a name applied, it seems, to the stick ta-mahn-a-

wis, or spirits of the woods which are accredited with the power to change people into toads, birds, beasts, etc., and keep them as long as they like, or until
they see fit to return them to their proper form.

People there are infected with the evil eye, in the imagination of the Indian,
and such they always try to avoid—especially so with children, and hence a
charm in the form of a rattle was always provided to hang over the bed or
cradle of the child. If a person entered the room and made pleasant with the
child, and took the rattle, all well and good. If he avoided the child and rattle and acted suspiciously, look out for him—he was one possessed of the evil
eye, and was cultus.

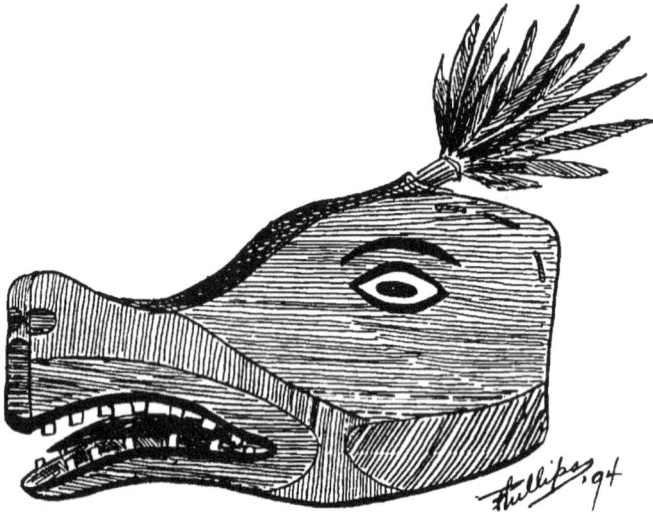

Wolf-mask—Used in the ceremony of the Black Ta-mahn-a-wis by the Skokomish
or Twana Indians

Such persons were invested, in the Indian mind, with the spirit power, and
through the influence of this evil eye men and children were wrought upon by
the Skal-lal-a-toot and changed to various forms of birds, beasts, trees, stones,
etc. These evil-eyed geniuses were able to exert this influence for bad to
great distances, from the Sound to the Columbia river, and infect individuals
there with its baneful influence, the same as if they were by their side.

The Indians used in this connection a mask, which might be called the crying mask, for it seems to have been used as a kind of "Winslow's soothing

syrup" to make the children stop crying. A representation of one of these masks made out of cedar wood and still in good preservation is shown in a sketch herein. The mask is nothing more than a flat board-like piece, longer than the ordinary shingle, with the face cut into it by a series of holes. It was placed in front of the person's face, and the mother or person using it would suddenly appear before the child to be quieted, singing a peculiar monotone song. It was simply a repetition of the word "skal-lay-a, skal-lay-a," with the last syllable drawn out indefinitely. Doubtless the charm worked well, and such practices probably had as much to do with the establishment of the seeds of superstition in the infantile mind as any after teaching could have had.

The Puget Sound Indian generally appears to have been but very slightly advanced in the art of carving and what work that is left is of a very crude workmanship. A few good specimens are found among them but it is questionable if any of them are original. In the illustrations is the rude carving of the bear totem on the stem of a canoe found among the Skokomish Indians, though the canoe might have come from the northern Indians who followed more closely the practice of decoration of the canoe.

In comparison to this is shown a carving, the figurehead of the old bark Enterprise which has lain a wreck on the beach at Agate pass, near the Old-Man-House reservation, Port Madison, since some time in the early 50's. This figurehead was removed from the old hulk and is now among the Indian relics of the old pioneer, William Deshaw. The carving is the work of native East Indians, according to the story of the skipper of the old bark. He came with his vessel from Calcutta to Puget Sound, and while in a port of East India went out with the nobility on a tiger hunt. Securing one, he expressed a desire to have a carving of the head for his vessel in honor of the hunt, and by direction of the rajah or some other high potentate it was made for him by the natives. It is of teak wood and well preserved and hard as flint almost. The figurehead was adorned with large eyes of pearl which after the old bark was wrecked were removed. When the captain expressed a desire to have a tiger head like the animal killed, the Indians set to work and in just two weeks had it completed and at the vessel when it was put on. A good story was told by William Deshaw on Mr. Meigs, the mill owner, at the time the old bark fell to pieces while lying at the mill wharf. It was a calm day, no wind, but the bark all of a sudden went to pieces from sheer age. The mizzen mast went by the board on the very day that Mr. Meigs was in Seattle getting insurance on the vessel as he had just about concluded a purchase of her. Meigs returned to the mill that evening and seeing the wreck said to her old skipper: "Well, I guess you'd better get that old hulk out of here or it will be tearing down of my wharf." They started in to get the old hulk away from the wharf and she was hauled across the narrow stretch of water onto the beach. As the tide went out she careened over and as Deshaw says, "just naturally wilted away." The old bark still lies on the beach where she was left twenty-five years or more ago, and the sand has drifted in and about her till it is in places eight and ten feet deep and she is almost lost to view.

The face mask shown in the illustrations herewith, now hangs on the walls of Wm. Deshaw's store at Agate pass and was given him many years ago by a chief from the straits tribes, and was given with the assurance that it was one of the most powerful charms the Indians possessed. It was particularly efficacious in keeping off the "evil eye" and all that was necessary to be done was

WOLF-MASK—Made by Skokomish Indians, now in possession of Rev. Myron Eels

to keep it hung up where everyone who entered the building could see it as he entered. If the person entering was possessed of the evil eye, after seeing it he would be powerless to do any evil.

Deshaw had performed a great kindness for the Indian, and had won his everlasting gratitude. The Indian had no money, nor could money have bought the charmed mask, but he gave it up in return for the kindness of saving his daughter's life.

One day a band of the Indians had come up sound and camped on the beach at the reservation for a few days. While there an Indian daughter of the chief got sick and a terrible hubbub was raised by the Indians in their efforts to drive away the evil eye that had fallen upon her. The medicine men exhausted

all their powers and could not bring her around. Deshaw went across the
passage to see what all the noise was about and found the girl stripped and
lying on a mat on the beach with the medicine men beating her body with hot
rocks. Blood was oozing from her ears and nostrils and she was almost dead.
He quickly drove the medicine men away, had her wrapped in blankets and
carried across the water to his trading post. Here proper treatment and medicine brought her around and in a day or two she was in swimming as lively as
any of the other children. Before leaving the old chief went to see Deshaw,
told him he was poor and had no money, but some day would come and give
him something. Time passed, and when another year had rolled around, one
day there walked into the trading post an Indian with something rolled up
under his arm. The bundle was neatly wrapped up in a lot of skins, there
being a beaver, marten and silver gray fox skin among them. Deshaw had
forgotten the circumstance of the sick child and forgotten the man, but thought
he had seen him at some previous time. Watching his opportunity, the old
chief took the white man off to one side and recalled the incident and gave him
the mask, and told him what it was and what to do with it. Deshaw followed
instructions and apparently the mask has served its purpose well. "The evil
eye" has remained aloof from the trading post, and it looks as if, like the old
bark above referred to, it and its genial proprietor will continue to jog on down
Time's broad way until they fall to pieces together, "just naturally wilt
away."

The totem on page 41 was one very efficacious in their superstitions regarding children. It was given to Deshaw in 1861 by Charley G'Klobet, an Indian
of prominence in the early days. It was the guardian spirit of children before
mentioned herein. The medicine men, who were supposed to get their powers
from it would not part with one of them to save their life, so deep and strong
was their superstitious belief in regard to it. In their incantations over it they
would kneel before it at night on mats spread out, and with their long, greasy
hair done up in weird and fanciful knots, their face and bodies painted and
besmeared with paints, run around it, talking to it, praying to it and caressing
it until they, in their over-wrought imaginations had imbibed all the information it possessed in regard to the children.

The totem has a long nose, over-hanging brow, two big bead eyes, with
streaks of white paint across the face half way between the eyes and mouth.
There are daubs of blue paint all about the mouth and chin and a small streak
of blue around the neck. There is a circle on the breast cut with a knife and
radiating from the two upper arcs are small three-pronged notches cut in by
the same process much resembling a bird's claw and intended to represent the
superstition of the great white eagle, from which, and a great whale, the
Indians there are said to have sprung.

CHAPTER X

The religion of the Siwash is spiritualism pure and simple. Every tree and shrub, beast, bird or fish had its spirit, and every mountain was the abode of invisible gods who rode on the winds and clouds.

The existence of a supreme being or spirit was prevalent in the untutored minds of the aboriginal inhabitants of Puget Sound. They believed in it, yet never worshiped it, and never made much practical use of this belief. They believed in the devil or a spirit answering to that dreaded, though invisible monster, yet in their simple daily life there were intermediate spirits far more potent for good or evil to the minds of these dusky people. They laid strong hold of the power for good of an individual, independent spirit for each and every inhabitant, a sacred, protecting star through life, and no circumstances or conditions seem ever to have been strong enough to cause a violation of the sacred tenets of that religion. Every Indian possessed a guardian spirit of his own. This was supposed to watch over him, protect him from the evil spirits that filled the woods and the air, and as long as it was kept inviolate was the one beaming, assuring aud ever-present guardianship of the Indian life.

When of youthful age—12 or 13 years—the Siwash would betake themselves to the woods, to an isolation as deep and perfect as that of Elisha in the cave in the forest attended by his ministering ravens. There a process of purification, almost of sanctification, would be submitted to, continuing from eight to thirteen days, or as long as the physical powers of the Indian could bear up under it. They refrained from eating, and practiced a self-imposed bodily chastening, until the extreme of physical suffering and mental anguish and over-excitement being reached, the Indian mind was in a condition to believe anything or see in the solitude about him any beast, bird or spirit the freaks of the overwrought imagination might conjure up.

That settled it. The first object, be that beast or bird, that passed before his vision and reflected in his diseased mind, was ever after sacred to him. The spell was broken and the Indian hied himself away to his fellows, happy and ready to stand among his tribe a favored individual. In their hunts and migrations that beast or fowl was never molested by that Indian. Others might kill or conquer, but he, never. It followed him through life, and was believed to exert a great power for good.

The traditions, superstitions and fetish practices of the early Indians of Skokomish and Old-Man-House as well of the Sound seem to blend and intermingle in such a way that it is almost impossible to clearly define them. Only deep and continued study can avail to get a proper understanding of them. Of their traditions the greatest seems to have been that of Do-ka-batl, a great spirit, whose peculiar powers lay in his ability to change big and little mortals into any kind of a beast, bird or stone or thing that his fancy dictated. Under

BOWL AND SPOON OF MOUNTAIN SHEEP HORN—TWANAS

such conditions it could not be otherwise than that very great respect should be shown to this masterful spirit, and respect and reverence for it seems to have been rather than fear and trembling.

The tradition of Do-ka-batl among the Twana or Skokomish Indians is alive to-day and they have always maintained that the great spirit was a woman, while the tribes north of them hold to the belief that it was a man.

At any rate Do-ka-batl made a great sensation when he or she first took it in mind to go abroad among the tribes that infested the Sound. The coming

was like a great big cloud that overspread the whole sky.   He came up out of
the sea, way over in the southwest from the direction of the Gray's harbor
country.   It does not appear that Do-ka-batl came with great noise and tumult,
with rattling of thunder, or peal of lightning, but like the great, even tempered spirit that he was; he came like an angel of peace to teach the people
good things.   He found the Twana Indian ancestors trying to catch fish in
Hood's canal with their hands.   Do-ka-batl taught them how to make traps
and stretch them across the river and waters and take great quantities of fish,
and so the Indians after that had life easy and lived in contentment and with
little labor.

Then, it was a very, very long time ago, there were not deer to run the
woods, nor humming birds to make music with their little wings, no pretty
blue jays to go cawing among the trees and a great many other useful and
ornamental things of nature had not any being.   Do-ka-batl provided for all
these, though it must be said that a great many naughty Indians were sacrificed in order to bring it about.   Their tradition of Do-ka-batl's transformation
of the deer is much like that of many other of the Indian tribes.

The great spirit on his visit came across a worthless fellow one day who was
making sharp the edge of a knife, probably a very different affair from the
steel knife of to-day.   The great spirit said :

"What are you doing there ?"   This in the Twana dialect, of course.

The worthless fellow replied, " Nothing," also in Indian.

The Do-ka-batl replied :   "I know what you are doing ; you are going to
kill me.   Give me that knife."

The Indian was frightened but gave up the knife and turned to run, but as
he did so the great spirit stuck it in his heel and the Indian began to jump
about and he has been jumping about ever since in the shape of a deer, for he
was quickly transformed into one as soon as the knife entered his heel.   The
little hoof that sticks out of the deer's foot just above the two main hoof toes
and at the back is the handle of the knife that Do-ka-batl stuck there.

While among the Twanas Do-ka-batl came across another fellow flopping his
hands over his head much like a donkey does his ears when keeping the gnats
and flies out of his eyes.   The Indian, however, was trying to keep off the
rain.   Do-ka-batl thought that a fellow who was afraid of getting wet was no
good, so he changed him into a humming bird while he was still at the foolish
pastime, and the Indians say that is why the humming bird always keeps its
wings going.   The Indian when changed did not stop his foolish flopping of
his hands, but kept right on.

One day, while Do-ka-batl tarried among them they were at their ta-mahn-
a-wis, and one of their medicine men, probably all of them, had his shock of
black greasy hair done up in a top-knot on the top of his head.   This angered

Do-ka-batl and he thought such an Indian would be more useful in the form of a pretty bird, so he changed him into a blue jay, with his top-knot still tied up on the top of his head. That is why the blue jay wears his hair pompadour. The grating sound of the blue jay's voice probably is a reproduction of the medicine man's song at the time, though this does not form a part of the tradition.

There is a very pretty tradition among the Indians at the Skokomish reservation about the origin of the big marsh lands at the mouth of that river. A vast reed-grown area blocks up the river to-day and it is a great place for all kinds of water fowl and the like. Cat-tails grow there enough for all the rush mats of the entire Indian population, so that while Do-ka-batl under the guise of his wrath made a great transformation that brought lasting good to the red faced people. When Do-ka-batl left the Twana village at the mouth of the Skokomish to continue his journey on down the beautiful shores of the canal his big foot slipped from under him at the edge of the water and he fell.

This made him angry and he cursed the ground, and, lo; the water went away and a great mass of ground rose up, half sea half land, and so it is to this day. The pretty cat-tails and tula grass came up over the ground and the ducks and geese came and made their nests and gathered the tender shoots and leaves of the sea-weed for food. Had it been any other great spirit than Do-ka-batl he might have placed a curse on the people of the Indian village rather than on the ground, but he did not and they have lived and prospered ever since. Though their number is small to-day they have the best gardens and fields and orchards and houses of all the Indian people on the Sound. Do-ka-batl continued his journey down the canal after getting upon his feet again and to this day the Indians still point to the marks in the rocks along the beach made by his big feet. There are two big prints a few miles from the beach close to what is now Hoodsport, which have vague resemblance to a mammoth foot-print, and these the Indians say were made by Do-ka-batl.

Their traditional story of the deluge is much like that told by some of the eastern tribes, excepting as to canoes which, of course, the Indians here used to ascend to the top of their biggest mountains instead of going up horse-back. With the Twana Indians they did not succeed in getting onto the highest mountain, but on one much less in height. The big waters kept creeping up the mountain sides and as the Indians had neglected to tie their canoes many of them were swept away and carried down to the mouth of the Columbia river, and there the survivors waited until the floods abated, and formed another tribe.

Some very long cedar bark canoes remained to the Indians, however. Do-ka-batl, or some other good and friendly spirit, however, must have been about to look after the Twana Indians, for the waters acted as if they were not allowed to engulf the Indians on the lower mountains. Instead of presenting a level plane the waters took the position of an inclined plane, reaching from the top of the higher mountain which they engulfed down to the peak of the lower one, whose top was not covered, and so the Indians were saved. These mountains, in the tradition, were far to the northeast or east from the site of the Twana Indian village and the Indians traveled a long time in their canoes to reach them.

One day an Indian lad was going with his gourd for water. The boy or the water he was carrying was making a "chug, chug, chug" noise, that sounded much like the song of the turtledove nowadays. The Do·ka-batl was near at the time and not liking the noise he transformed the Indian boy into a dove and sent him off into the woods to sing away his life in solitude, and that is why the song of the turtledove can be heard floating out in summer days from among the green branches and woods of the forests.

THE GAME OF SING GAMBLE—SKOKOMISH TRIBE.

CHAPTER XI

There are still many practices of the early Indians continued through the present generation of half civilized and half-blood descendants. The Indian has an inveterate love of gambling. Indeed, the Indian life is all a game of chance, so superstitious a being is he. They probably have gambled ever since the days of the first Indian. Among the games is that of "sing-gamble," which though divested of much of its old-time ceremony, is still the great game of chance among them. In its simple form it is but a plain game of guessing with the chances equally for or against the players. The Indians, however, believe in it with all their soul and they will throw their whole soul into it to-day as they will risk their all, horses, dogs, canoes, jewelry, almost their wives and children upon its infatuous chances. The preparation and ceremony formerly attendant upon it is what gave to the game its great renown. To-day when played with more than a dozen persons it is still a game of great moment. The writer, who recently visited the Skokomish Indians had the pleasure of witnessing a "sing-gamble," which lasted almost an entire night, though but a few took part. The illustration accompanying this story is a good representation of the scene, as it is an exact likeness of the half-breed and full-blood Indians who participated. Night time, that lends the most weirdness, is chosen as the time for the "sing-gamble."

In brief, a huge fire was built, on either side of which a long board was laid down on a shorter piece, so that they might be said to represent the strings of a violin. The players ranged themselves back of the boards in two opposing sides. The gambling paraphernalia consisted of several sticks of green alder with the bark peeled off, excepting some that had a little ring of bark left around the middle of the stick. Counters for the game were secured in the shape of sharpened cedar sticks, which were set in the ground on either side of the fire in front of the players. In that instance 30 points constituted the game, though it is often run up to 60. Preliminary to the start the bets had to be arranged between the players. Two canoes, a silver watch, two ponies, $1.50 in silver, a coat, a shirt and some other things were wagered on the result. This preliminary took up a great deal of time and much talking, but was finally adjusted to the satisfaction of all. Then the game began.

Two of the players on one side selected each two of the alder sticks, which were about four inches long and an inch in diameter. Each man took one clean of bark and one with the circle of bark left in the middle, that was the distinguishing mark. The point to be detected by the opposing side was which hand held the clean stick or which the one with the bark on it. First the two Indians having the sticks fumbled with them under their shirts, then they brought them forth and the music began, all the Indians on that side joining in and at the same time those not holding the sticks keeping time by rapping on the board in front of them with long sticks of hard wood. The music, if such it could be called, was rapid and vociferous, a kind of sing-song monotone drawling affair, which at times changed to something very like a rude melody.

All this time the two players were swinging their hands at half arm, bending at the elbow, in front of them, while they leaned far forward with their bodies, anon at times throwing their heads back and their chests out and all the time keeping up that dreadful, unearthly singing. Occasionally they would dextrously throw the short sticks in the air, catch them again and slap them under their shirts, bring them forth again, all the time keeping up with the procession of noise and the motions of their bodies.

The more pandemonium, the more hurrah the harder it was supposed to be for the opponents to guess the proper hand that held the bark-ringed stick.

Whenever an opponent made a guess he quickly threw out one hand to arm's length in a pointing way, while with the other he made a fanning motion in a half circle, placing the palm of the hand over the other arm at about the elbow. Practice makes this a very graceful motion. The singing and noise ceases and the player opens up his hands. If the other has guessed rightly, the two sticks are tossed across the fire and the other side takes them up while the men just losing them become the guessers. Two Indians do the playing while two are selected on the other side to do the guessing. Whenever one side makes a point, which consists in a failure of the opponents to guess rightly, they mark it up by sticking one of the cedar sticks into the ground in front of them. When they lose they pull one out.

This game lasted from about 9 in the evening until 3 in the morning, and before it ended the Indians were nearly exhausted from their excessive singing and excited motions. Sweat poured off some of them in streams during the performance, and they divested themselves of everything but trousers and shirt. Some became very hoarse from the singing. Many of them rode to the scene on their ponies from distances of several miles and next day it was one of the topics of the reservation.

CHAPTER XII

The Rev. Myron Eells, who for a score of years has been a missionary among the Indians of Puget Sound, has made investigations into the myths and traditions of the people among whom he has labored, and has stored up many an interesting story of the Thunderbird superstition. He says:

The general idea among the Indians is that thunder is caused by an immense bird, whose size darkens the heavens, whose body is the thunder cloud, the flapping of whose wings causes the thunder, and the bolts of fire, which it sends out of its mouth to kill the whale for its food, are the lightning. The Makahs and some other tribes, however, invest the animal with a twofold character, human and bird-like. According to them the being is supposed to be a gigantic Indian, named in the dialects of the various coast tribes Kakaitch, T'hlu-kluts, and Tu-tutsh, the latter being the Nootkan name. He lives in the highest mountains and his food consists of whales. When he goes after food he puts on a great garment, which is made of a bird's head, a pair of very large wings, and a feather covering for his body, and around his waist he ties the lightning fish, which slightly resembles the sea horse. This animal has a head as sharp as a knife, and when he sees a whale he darts the lightning fish into its body, which he then seizes and carries to his home. Occasionally, however, he strikes a tree, and more seldom a man.

The origin of the bird, according to Mr. Swan, as given by the Chehalis and Chinook Indians, is as follows: "Ages ago an old man named Too-lux, or the south wind, while traveling north, met an old woman named Quoots-hooi, who was an ogress or giantess. He asked her for food, when she gave him a net, telling him that she had nothing to eat, and he must go and try to catch some fish. He accordingly dragged the net and succeeded in catching the grampus, or, as the Indians called it, a little whale. This he was about to cut with his knife, when an old woman cried out to him to take a sharp shell and not to cut the fish crossways, but split it down the back. Without giving heed to what she said he cut the fish across the side and was about to take off a piece of blubber, but the fish immediately changed into an immense bird, that, when flying,

54

completely obscured the sun, and the noise made by its wings shook the earth.''
They also add that this Thunderbird flew to the north and lit on the top of the
Saddleback mountain, near the Columbia river, where it laid a nest full of eggs.
It was followed by the giantess, who found the eggs; whereupon she began to
break and eat them, and from these mankind, or at least the Chehalis and Chinook tribes, were produced. The Thunderbird, called Hahness by those Indians,
came back, and, finding its nest destroyed, went to Too-lux, the south wind,

THE THUNDERBIRD MASK—TWANAS

for redress, but neither of them could ever find the ogress, although they regularly went north every year.

As to the cause of thunder among these tribes Mr. Swan says that when a young girl reaches womanhood she has to go through a process of purification, which lasts a month. Among other customs at this time, if there is a southwest wind, with signs of rain, she must on no account go out of doors, else the southwest wind is so offended that he will send the Thunderbird, who then, by shaking his wings, causes the thunder, and from whose eyes go forth the flashes of lightning. As far as Mr. Swan knew, every thunder storm which occurred while he lived at Shoalwater Bay (three years) was attributed by the Indians to this cause—that is, to some girl disobeying this law.

The Indians are very superstitious in regard to this bird, believing that if they possess any feather, bone or other part of it, or bone of the lightning fish, it will be of supernatural advantage to them. A Makah, who had been very sick, was reduced to a skeleton, and it was believed could not recover, yet he managed to crawl one day, says Mr. Swan, to a brook near by, and while there he heard a rustling which so frightened him that he covered his face with his blanket. Peeping out he saw a raven near him, apparently trying to throw up something, and, according to the Indian, it did throw up a piece of bone about three inches long. The Indian secured this, believing it to be a bone of the Thunderbird, and he was told by the Indian doctors that it was a medicine sent to him by his Ta-mahn-a-wis, or guardian spirit, to cure him. It was a fact that he did recover very quickly, perhaps through the effect of his imagining it to be such a bone and a strong medicine. It may also have been dropped by the raven.

On one occasion, at a display of fireworks in Port Townsend, a number of rockets bursting showed fiery serpents. These the Indians believed belonged to the Thunderbird, and offered large sums for pieces of the animal. They told Mr. Swan they would give two hundred dollars for a backbone of one.

A Quiniault Indian once professed to have obtained a feather of one of these birds. He said he saw one of them light, and, creeping up softly, tied a buckskin string to one of its feathers and fastened the other end to a stump. When the bird flew away it left the feather, which was forty fathoms long. No other Indian saw it, for he was careful to keep it hid, but possession of it was not questioned by the rest, as he was very successful in catching sea otter. According to the Makahs, one of the principal homes of the bird is on a mountain back of Clayoquot, on Vancouver island, where is a lake, and around it the Indians say are many bones of whales which the bird has killed.

Many of the northwestern Indians have a performance in honor of this Thunderbird, which is called the thunderbird performance or "black ta-mahn-a-wis." It is said to have originated with the Nittinat Indians, according to the following legend, as recorded by Mr. Swan: Two men had fallen in love with the same woman, but she would not give either the preference, whereupon they began to quarrel. But one of them, of more sense than the other, said: "Do not let us fight about that squaw. I will go and see the chief of the wolves and he will tell me what is to be done, but I cannot get to his house except by stratagem. Now, they will know we are at variance; so do you take me by the hair and drag me over these sharp rocks, which are covered with barnacles, and I shall bleed and pretend to be dead, and the wolves will come and carry me away to their house." This was done, but when the wolves were ready to eat him he jumped up and astonished them by his boldness. The chief wolf was so much pleased with his bravery that he taught the man the mysteries of the Thunderbird performance. This, the most savage of all the Indian ceremonies, spread among all the Indians on Puget Sound, as well as to the north, the latter being the most savage in the performance of the ceremonies. Among other things, the performers hoot like owls, howl like wolves, paint their bodies black, especially the face, from which fact, in whole or in part, comes the English name "black tamahnawis;" scarify their arms, legs and sometimes the body, so as to bleed profusely, in remembrance of its origin; they make much noise by firing guns, pound on drums to represent thunder, flash torches of pitchwood about as a representation of lightning, and whistle sharply in imitation of the wind. The ceremonies, however, vary in different tribes, being much more savage and bloody in some than in others. Among the Makahs five days are usually occupied in secret ceremonies, such as initiating candidates and other performances, before any public outdoor ceremonies take place. Among the Clallams the candidate for initiation is put into a kind of mesmeric sleep, which does not appear to be the case with the Makahs. Among the Clallams, however, the secret ceremonies are not always as long as among the Makahs.

CHAPTER XIII

Superstition was born with the first man, and is about the only thing in the world that remains unchanged today. The more ignorant the people the deeper we find them plunged into the dark maze of the mythical. People of highly civilized nations are not free from this clinging shadow of the forgotten or un-known past, and, although they laugh at the idea as being rank foolishness, they will feel a little shiver if they are the first to cross the track of a funeral, or they will stop and pick up a pin which points toward them on the sidewalk, not because they need it, but because—well, just because they want to. Civil-ized people call this trait an eccentricity in themselves and superstition in the savage.

Savages the world over are steeped in superstitious myths, traditions and in folk-lore which is peculiar each to its own tribe, or clan, but through it all there are threads which connect one tribe or people with another, though miles of distance may intervene.

The stories vary in detail and in the telling, but the main points are identical, showing conslusively that at some pre-historic time men had a means of inter-communication without telegraph, ships or railroads, and that a myth origin-ated by the medicine men or prophets of one tribe or nation would spread far beyond the boundaries of the tribe which first practiced it.

There are today two remarkable instances of this fact, both semi-religious and both originating with the medicine men.

The first is the ghost dance, made vaguely familiar by the battle of Wounded Knee some years ago in the Dakota Bad Land. The other is the myth of the Thunderbird, the Skam-son of the Haidas, and known from Cape Flattery to Wisconsin by various tribal names.

The object of this chapter is to show the remarkable hold which a mythical tale can get on the savage mind, and how the Ta-mahn-a-wis sway the people of their tribe by their dark practices; hence the myth of the Thunderbird as believed in by them from the coast to the great lakes.

The tale involving the origin of this strange creature has already been given as it is told among the Twanas, but it is more than probable that each tribe has its own version of the first appearance of it in their horizon, as all Indians believe in a multitude of spirits, both good and bad.

The idea of a Great Spirit as is generally taken by whites to cover the Indian religion is erroneous, as every mountain, river, lake or other natural object, as well as natural phenomenon, is accredited with being the home of some particular spirit; in fact, the old Greek mythology is a good comparison, and illustrates the idea exactly.

Hence we find the thunder personified by an immense bird with some tribes, and with others as half bird, half man, or a man who wears a bird's skin, but, all agree that the personage is of collossal proportions, and give it the name of Thunderbird.

Surroundings modify the form and features of this mythical being to a great extent, and account for the different descriptions of it given by different tribes.

The Twanas believe it to be an immense bird which lives on the top of a high mountain, and feeds on whales which it kills by lightning. It is here in the form of an eagle, with quill feathers sixty fathoms long in each wing.

With them it is a good spirit, harming no one unless an individual has displeased it; then the person is killed by a glance from its eye, which is the lightning. They believe that it is the god of rain, and also that the image of it carved on their implements of war or the chase gives the owner strength in fighting and good luck in hunting. Thus it is a hunter-warrior-rain god. Rev. Eells reports a carving of the Twana version cut in a basaltic boulder near Eniti, Wash., which the Indians say is the face of the Thunderbird, and they believe that if the rock is shaken or removed in any way it will cause rain.

DAKOTA DESIGNS OF SMALLER THUNDERERS.

Among the Haidas of Queen Charlotte island it is believed to be an immense creature, half man, half bird, whose body is the mountains to the sea, shielded from view by heavy clouds, the main difference in the story being in the lightning, which is here personified by the fish instead of described as a glance of the eye of the bird covered with feathers, and who is accompanied by the lightning fish, which he darts at the whales and kills them for food. This lightning fish is pictured as the Killer whale, which is feared by the Indians, as it attacks them sometimes while voyaging about in their canoes; hence they credit it as a companion of the Thunderbird, or Skam-son, as they call it. As with the Twanas, the thunder is caused by the flapping of the wings as the creature flies from Skam-son. This is easily accounted for by the fact that the Haidas are a sea-going nation, a nation of fishermen, who gain their living from the ocean; hence they would naturally associate a fish of some kind with any tradition or myth where it could be used.

They tattoo the image of the bird on their bodies as a clan or family mark in the same manner as they do the otter, halibut, skate and other designs, to signify the family the individual belongs to; or, as one remarked to Judge Swan of Port Townsend: "If you had the image of a swan tattooed on your body the Indians would know your family name."

The figure is carved on their totem posts and canoe stems and painted on the house fronts, and various implements with the belief, as among the Twanas, that it gives them power, courage and luck in hunting, fishing or war. A mask representing the head of the bird is worn in the Ta-mahn-a-wis dances and ceremonies, which have something to do with the Thunderbird, though just what this is has never been clearly ascertained, as the Indians will not allow whites to witness these Ta-mahn-a-wis practices, which are of the nature of a secret society among civilized people.

The Twanas and the Clallams also use a mask of a different design for the same purposes. No tribes tattoo the figure on their person, so far as known, outside of the Haidas.

Leaving the coast and going eastward we find the Thunderbird among the Sioux of Dakota and Eastern Montana again, this time being personified in an immense eagle, with four joints to the wing and which dwells in a lodge on the top of a high knoll or butte. The lodge has four doors, one for each cardinal point of the compass, and at each door there is a guardian spirit. These spirits are a beaver, a butterfly, an otter and one other animal not clearly defined, whose duty it is to guard and act as messengers for the Thunderbird.

OJIBWA FLYING THUNDERBIRD

As with the Twanas, the lightning is a glance from the eye, and a person who has a presentment that the Thunderbird is displeased with him and intends to kill him, retires to a high hill to await his doom, after having bid his friends farewell. Sometimes, owing to the isolated position of the individual, he is actually struck by lightning during some of the heavy thunder storms of the region, and that settles the myth all the firmer in the Indian mind, for the Thunderbird it was who killed him, just as he said it would.

Here the myth assumes three or four, or rather a family of thunderers, some good, some evil, some who guard the destiny of the warrior and strike terror into the heart of the enemy, others who see that the hunter does not come home empty handed.

Some are headless and have wings, some are wingless but provided with heads, but the Thunderbird, with a big "T," who is the rain god and thunder creater and good spirit-in-chief, is described as a very large bird which flies fast. This bird has a whole brood of little ones, who follow behind the big thunderer and make the long rumble noticeable in the prairie thunder peals. The old bird is wise and good, harming no one, and causing rain, which makes the plants grow, but the young ones are like young men, very mischievous, and will not listen to counsel and are continually doing a great deal of damage, and killing an occasional person purely in a playful way, for when they grow old, they settle down and become good spirits, too. Nothing can kill or destroy the Thunderbird but an immense giant, who can stride over rivers and mountains and can kill anything by a look. This giant still exists, but nobody knows where, and is always hunting for the thunderer, who has to fly from place to place to keep away from the evil giant, thus causing storms by flying about. The old bird starts with the loud crash of noise, and then the little ones rise in a swarm and make a lot more noise, but not so loud as the old one, which flies very fast.

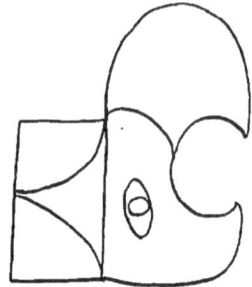

HAIDA TATOOING — THUNDERBIRD HEAD.

The giant killed one of the old ones a long, long time ago, back of Little Crow's village, near the head of the Mississippi river, and the medicine men still have totems made of the feathers and bones, and they are very strong medicine against evil.

This bird had "a face like a man, nose like an eagle bill, body long and slender and four joints to each wing, which were painted zigzag like the lightning, and the back of the head was rough and red, according to the Dakota tradition. This is the Sioux story of the Thunderbird. Going a little further east we find the Ojibwa, who live in Minnesota and around the shores of Lake Superior with a myth of the thunderer which makes it entirely a good spirit, a sort of servant of the medicine man, shaman or priest, and who helps them to work cures, find good medicine plants, and many other things which have a good influence.

With the Ojibwa it is also an immense eagle-like bird but without any superfluity of wing joints. The thunder is the noise of its flying and it causes rain which makes medicine plants grow and also it can apparently find a medicine plant to fit the particular disease by looking on the earth, in the sky or in the inside of the earth, either of which places it can visit at will under the instructions of the medicine man or shaman, who holds a controlling power over it.

There is no record of any masks being used to represent the thunderer, directly east of the coast tribes, the only representations being from Indian drawings, which interpret their idea and which are represented in this book.

There are no carvings or images except those worked in beads, from near Fort Snelling, Minnesota, which represent the bird with the red breast and tail, and having somewhat of an eagle form.

The Ojibwa figúres are from drawings on the "music board" used by the Ojibwa at the initiation of candidates into the society of the Mide-wiwin or great medicine, and are really notes in the medicine song of this society, for they are only one of numerous characters painted in rows on a board which are translated into a chant by the Mide men to mean some particular achievement of the Thunderbird under the guidance of that society.

This Thunderbird lives somewhere up in the sky and can only be brought to the earth by the Mide or shaman priests, who are the medicine men of the tribe, and members of the Mide-wiwin society, and then only to serve some good end in the making of medicine.

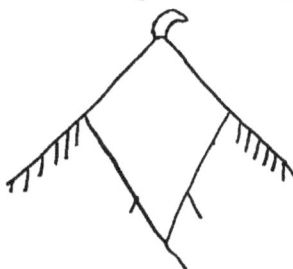

OJIBWA THUNDERER

Thus the Thunderbird of the Pacific Coast degenerates into a servant of the Ojibwa medicine man, or else the servant grows to the proportion of a God as he travels West according to which version is taken as to the origin, but it is likely that the servant grew to be the God, as all tales grow in the telling, especially among an ignorant people like the Indians.

Most of these myths and folk-lore tales have their origin in a "dream" or trance of some medicine man whose word is taken without question by his people because he is really a religious magician or prophet-doctor who is credited with many supernatural powers, has "visions" and foretells events. They are clever in the means they employ to bring about a desired end and thus "speak a single, straight tongue" to their people who would as soon cut off a hand as to doubt the statements of the Ta-mahn-a-wis men. With this kind of a power wielded over them it is no wonder that the simple-minded Indian peoples the earth, the sea and the air with all kinds of demons of which the Thunderbird is but one example, and has a noise for every Skal-lal-a-toot, and a Skal-lal-a-toot for every noise, with spirits inhabiting everything, totems, fetiches and charms for and against a thousand and one things which he does not understand and credits to the supernatural.

CHAPTER XIV

The illustrations of the Puget Sound Indian accompanying are very characteristic of the race. In the main the general characteristics are such that they cannot be mistaken. The infusion of white and foreign blood during the last 30 years or so has had a marked effect upon the later generation and to a great extent changed the current of Indian life. Leaving out of the question the general features of color and vigorousness of form they are readily distinguishable from the pure bloods about them. Half-breeds more readily fall into and adopt the customs and practices of the whites and to a considerable extent are not averse to manual labor. Hence they are found in the mills and forests of the country sharing the burdens of civilized life.

But work for a genuine Siwash is no more palatable than it is to a Patagonian. He sticks to his " canim " like a leech to the epidermis. Laziness is a cultivated characteristic of the old-time Indian, is grafted into his being as indelibly as the tattooing on the arm of an East India man and he will never work so long as the sands on his native beach contain a live clam or the hills above a huckleberry bush from which his klootchman can dig a bivalve or pick a wicker basket of blue berries. He will not even deign to assist in these simple labors, and in this he does not surpass his kinsman who are reared in the interior. These are the drudgery of his klootchman and night or day, sun or rain, she may always be found on the beach rustling up the next meal. He will sometimes accompany her and when there are two baskets to " tote " he may even consent to carry one, but it is much more to his nature to trudge along at the rear empty handed. This characteristic is more apparent in the cities when, having more of one or the other than the family larder requires for the time being, they seek the towns to dispose of it for a trifling sum, which is to be expended in knick knacks, gew gaws, etc., etc., that are the fancy of the Indian mind.

The one thing only which the old-time Siwash thinks it not beneath his dignity to indulge in is fishing, and this is his particular special privilege which he never permits any interference with. True, his dame has the privilege of fishing for cod and dogfish and the commoner species, but the taking of the

lordly salmon is never relegated to her. If he is one of the old-time Indians wrapped still in the superstitious beliefs of his ancestors, not only is she not permitted the pleasure of the chase for salmon, but she is never permitted to put her foot inside the salmon canim, nor is she ever allowed to touch the salmon line or hook. That would forever spoil either canoe or line from use by the imperious head of the household. These practices, while still in vogue among the more isolated villages, is not so strictly adhered to by Indians who almost daily come in contact with the whites, nor are these remnants of a superstitious race very widely known among their enlightened and civilized neighbors. A trip to any of the favorite fishing grounds about the Sound and a study of the life of the village will convince any one that were they suddenly removed from all influence of civilized life, the Indian of today is just as he was when the first white man's boat ploughed the gentle waters of the Sound. The thoroughbred Siwash will not even countenance the pretty gearing of the modern fisherman, but clings tenaciously to those articles fashioned by his own hand. He, however, will use the spoon in trolling, but it is one he has made himself from the metal and polished in his own way, swung from a bit of wire crooked and fashioned in his own odd fashion. His is an invention unprotected, yet he will never trouble himself about letters patent, for no white man can ever imitate his work successfully. There is something about it that seems to have a most unusual attraction for the finest and best, for a Siwash is seldom met with winter or summer, on a fishing expedition without one or more of the best fish the water contains.

They know just the hour, just the spot and place when and where to fish and seldom are seen trolling any other time. Trout a Siwash has no love for and never attempts to take. He may have his camp on a stream alive with the finest of the trout species, but he never molests them. A polluted dog salmon lying dead upon the sand bank is more preferable in his eyes and he will pick up one and walk away with the same grim satisfaction that he will after having speared or hooked a monster silver side, the king of the genus.

The klootchman is no less characteristic in appearance and features than the Siwash himself. They are decrepit in looks, bowed in form from the constant life-long use of the canim, prematurely old and unsociable as a black bear. There is if possible more superstition, more mystery to the klootchman than to her lordly partner. She never talks to the whites unless it is to offer for sale the fruit from the forest, the catch from the salt water or when around on begging expeditions, and of the latter there is little. The Siwash will stoop to outright begging, especially if he is a chief or has become debauched by associates with evil-minded whites, but his wife scarcely ever.

Labelle klootchman is both the pride of the family and the belle of the village, and on her is lavished all the fashion and vermillion of the sweet society of the natives. She dotes on loud colors and is noticeably proud of whatever she wears as long as it is bright and showy. She ages, however, like an autumn leaf and once past sweet sixteen she is relegated to the shades of ugliness and forgotten. Of all things, Indian, the hardest to determine would be the age of the pure blood Siwash or klootchman. They may be about 30 or may be 75, they all look alike after reaching the usual majority in years.

Outside the supplying of daily wants the only other task of the pure-blood Siwash is the building of his cedar canoes. Seldom is it that the whites get an opportunity of seeing this work in progress. It is most always done on or near the beach in out-of-the-way places and the old-fashioned Indian-made hand adz is as religiously adhered to as it ever was. The interior of the cedar log was originally cleared by burning, but occasionally they will now condescend to the use of a heavier instrument secured from the whites to get rid of the core. In trimming down, fashioning and finishing up the canoe the little bit of sharpened steel is, however, always used.

Early Indians, and for that matter all of the present day, entertained a righteous dread of photography. Electricity, the galvanic battery and the telegraph wires were things as dreadful to them as their imaginary Skal-lal-la-toot, that ranged the woods about their villages. They believe that these things are spirits of some kind that have been through the influence of the white man's Ta-mahn-a-wis or big medicines enslaved to the fellow who happens to possess the electrical appliance.

When the old trader, William Deshaw, who has been frequently mentioned in connection with Port Madison Indians, first came to Agate pass to look after the Indians there he took with him an old-fashioned galvanic battery. This mysterious instrument probably invested him, in the eyes of the simple savages, who had never before heard of such things, with greater power than anything else he could possibly have taken among them. It promoted him at once to the position of a great white Ta-mahn-a-wis, whose influence was never afterwards disputed. Soon after his appearance there and acquaintance with the Old-Man-House tribes the construction of the old Puget Sound Telegraph & Cable company's line was carried past their village and it became a thing of dreadful consequence to the Indians. They avoided it and feared it as they did the "evil eye." It was quite an impossible thing to ever get an Indian to lend a hand at replacing the wires in position when they happened to become broken down during the winter storms. Touch an electric wire ? They would sooner have suffered the loss of a hand under a chopping block.

The old trader tells of many amusing spectacles with the use of the old galvanic battery on some of the Indians. As before stated the practices of their severe superstitious rites often caused many of the Ta-mahn-a-wis men to fall into trance-like and comatose conditions, from which it was impossible, by any known Indian agency to arouse them. The old trader tells of one that occurred at Old-Man-House in which the efficacy of the old galvanic battery was proved to the Indians satisfaction with a vengeance. One of these old medicine men had after several days of unusual exertion and privation fallen into a comatose condition. Every art known to the other's Ta-mahn-a-wis had been exerted to no purpose and as a last resort the Indians had sent for the white Ta-mahn-a-wis living across the narrow pass. "So he's dead, is he?" inquired the trader of the Indians who went after him.

"Yes, he's dead. Indian Ta-mahn-a-wis no good for him," returned the couriers.

"Umph! yes, well white man's Ta-mahn-a-wis fetch him," said the trader and he went after the old battery. Going across he found the Indian lying on the floor of a hut upon the inevitable rush mat and to all intents and purposes dead as a mackerel, with a howling, prancing mob of his brethern about him.

The trader felt of him, but he was cold and bloodless without apparent pulse or life. He cleared a space about him and arranged his battery. The Indians becoming subdued watched the process with incredulity and stoical silence. The poles of the instrument were placed so that the full effect of the electric current would be most keenly felt, and then the operator turned it on with force enough to have broken up the nerve system of a dozen ordinary men. With a bound and a shriek the prostrate form was on his feet in an instant and so sudden was the transformation that half the onlookers were knocked down by the terrified and quickened medicine man by his wild leap into the air. He bolted for the door and took for the woods amidst the greatest consternation of his mourning friends. He did not return for some days, but the evil spirit that had been supposed to have taken possession of him was effectually squelched. After that there was no more incredulous smiles and looks when the galvanic battery was around.

This trader, who knew Seattle's famous old chief almost as a brother, says they had a great time trying to secure a photograph of him in the early days. There was but one small photograph gallery in Seattle at that time. Many days and weeks passed before the old settler could induce the chief even to go near the place. By degrees they got him in the building, but when he would see the muzzle of the camera pointed at him, he would invariably break away. One day the settlers went all the way to Fort Steilacoom and bought a new suit of soldiers clothes for him to be photographed in. The old chief was greatly pleased at such a compliment, but when he found there was to be a string to the proposition, a consideration in the way of submitting to be photographed, the settlers could do nothing further with him. In the language of the old trader, "That put a squibosh on the whole business."

At the next attempt to get the old fellow photographed somebody got him to "swilling" a little and managed to get the old fellow into the gallery. He was too much under the influence of the liquid to know what was being done, and the photographer got a shot at him. When the old chief came to his senses he was dreadfully outraged in feeling and said that he "didn't want any more shots at him." After that when looking through a picture book the old chief was very careful. The Indian's superstition led him to believe that men in a picture took the evil genius of the photograph, or the electric wire lurked to pounce out and enslave him.

SYMBOLIC DRAWING—Northern Indians

It may be interesting, and at this time something of a relief from the duller monotony of the pages preceeding, to give one of the characteristic legends which were current among the Indians when first the whites came among them. This may properly be termed the Siwash legend of the first frog, and gives the sad fate that befell a too ardent Indian lover.

"Many, many snows ago the Great Tyee of all lived upon the earth; the snows that have come and gone since then cannot well be counted by men. The Great Tyee was not only chief over man, but also over the birds, the fish and all the animals in the woods. All feared him and did his bidding.

"The Great Tyee had been very successful in his wars, and had subjugated all the chiefs but Clack-a-mas, a warrior who had long and well fought against the Great Tyee. At last both, growing tired of war, resolved to smoke the great peace pipe and bury the hatchet, and to more firmly cement their growing friendship the Great Tyee asked for and obtained the consent of Clack-a-mas to the marriage of his daughter Kla-Kla-Klack-Hah (the woman who talks) to Wah-Wah-Hoo, the Tyee's only son. But the Great Tyee's plans for the marriage of his son were destined to be nipped in the bud. Wah-Wah-Hoo had long and ardently loved a maiden of his own tribe, a daughter of one of the lesser chiefs. Hah-Hah had all those graces which go to make a woman charming, and she was as deeply in love with Wah-Wah-Hoo as he with her.

"It is easier to imagine than to depict the grief of the lovers when they learned the will of the Great Tyee. To Wah-Wah-Hoo it seemed that nothing was left him to do but to prepare for the wedding, which was to take place immediately. It had not as yet occurred to him to disobey the Great Tyee. Such a path was fraught with too much danger to be taken at once, and for the present no ray of hope penetrated through the dark cloud that had settled down and quenched the bright light of his and Hah-Hah's happiness.

"Daily the preparations for the marriage went on, and as the day of its consummation drew nearer Wah-Wah-Hoo became more and more reluctant to carry out the command of the Great Tyee. On the day before the wedding Hah-Hah, robed in her brightest skins, went to keep the last tryst with her recreant lover. They met in a grassy dell, sprinkled over with brightest wild flowers; but to the infatuated lover Hah-Hah was the loveliest flower of them all. Love stole away his reason, and, forgetful of his duty to the Great Tyee, his father, Wah-Wah-Hoo gathered Hah-Hah up in his arms and hurried away into the forest. They journeyed many suns into the somber woods and finally built themselves a shelter on the bank of a great river, where, forgetful of the wrath of the Great Tyee, they were happy.

"The wedding day dawned. Kla-Kla-Klack-Hah, robed in her best skins, stood waiting the coming of Wah-Wah-Hoo to claim and to carry off his bride. The minutes swiftly multiplied into hours until Clack-a-mas, deeply chagrined at the disdainful treatment of his daughter, sought an explanation of the Great Tyee. A search was immediately instituted for Wah-Wah-Hoo, and then, and not until then, was the flight of the lovers discovered.

"At once the Great Tyee ordered his swiftest runners and his best trailers to follow and to bring back his disobedient son. Swiftly they ran through the woods, searching long and far, but baffled at last, they were compelled to return to the Great Tyee with the story of their failure.

"Then the Great Tyee went out, and, seated upon the river bank, called about him the chiefs of all the animals in the woods and of the fishes in the sea and commanded them as they feared his anger to search for and to find his son. They, dreading his power, immediately set out upon their quest.

"The snake, squirming his way in and out among the berry patches, searched long and arduously for the lovers. The chief of the mosquitos, calling about him his band, who number more than the grains of sand on the sea shore, searched for and found the lovers; but the chief, remembering that when, in an inadvertent and hungry moment he had alighted upon Hah-Hah's cheek she had spared his life, ordered his band to disperse and to say nothing of the lovers. The squirrel, running up and down the trees hoarding his winter stores, kept watch that the lovers did not go by him unseen. The eagle, in ever-increasing circles, soared high above the land and kept a watchful eye that the lovers did not escape him. The chief of the wolves found them, but, remembering that Wah-Wah-Hoo had saved his life when caught in a trap, he, too, commanded his followers to say nothing of the lovers.

"Soon the chilling blasts of winter went whistling through the woods, and the ice king, seizing the earth in his stifling grasp, wrapped it in a mantle of snow. Hunger—grim, gaunt, unrelenting hunger—entered Wah-Wah-Hoo's wigwam, and stole from him that which he loved best of all, Hah-Hah. Wah-Wah-Hoo, looking for the last time upon his sweetheart, turned away and hurried to the big rock overlooking the swirling water of the river. There, singing his death song, he flung himself into the water. But Wah-Wah-Hoo was destined not to die. The chief of the fishes swallowed him, and, swimming to the spot where the Great Tyee was standing, spewed him forth upon the bank.

"The Great Tyee cursed his son and changed him into a frog, whose dismal croaking is now heard, telling his sad story to the sons of man and warning them to be obedient."

CHAPTER XVI

The man in the moon, among some of the tribes, has a very pretty story reserved for him, which like the young brave who was turned into a croaking frog was placed in the moon for his too ardent love for a dusky maiden. The legend more properly belongs to the Vancouver island tribes. The following version was told by an Indian who is thought to be over 100 years old and it is faithfully believed in by himself and his tribe :

" ' Many, many snows ago, long before a white man came to this country, there lived in a village on Quatsino sound the Great Tyee of all. He was not only tyee over men, but also over the animals, birds and fishes. His smile was like the sun coming from behind the cloud, his frown like the lightning, quick and awful, no man could stand before it and live.

" ' Wah-nah-ho, the Great Tyee's son, was just the opposite from his father, sunny tempered, and loved by every one. The animals and birds in the forest, the fishes in the sea, all loved and did his bidding. Now, Wah-nah-ho was unhapppy. He loved Tum-Tum, the fairest maiden in all the land, and the Great Tyee had commanded him to marry Shingoopoot's daughter, who was ugly, ill-tempered, and who had already had one husband. Now, Wah-nah-ho, who in all things else had been a most obedient son, rebelled against his father, and with Tum-Tum at night when all the village was asleep, stole away, and running swiftly, hid themselves in the forest.

" ' The Great Tyee, when he discovered the flight of the lovers, was very wroth, and swore that he would not show himself to his people until the couple were found and brought before him. All the young men of the tribe immediately plunged into the forest and hurried away to look for the lovers. They searched long and at a great distance, but unsuccessfully, and one by one returned to the village. Then the Great Tyee ordered all the animals and birds out of the forest, and all the fishes out of the rivers determined that hunger should compel his disobedient son to return.

" ' Finally, as day after day, he set his unsuccessful snares in the woods and searched the streams for food, Wah-nah-ho was at last driven to return to the village. He sought his father with his sweetheart, and on his knees told him of his love for Tum-Tum, and begged for forgiveness. The Great Tyee's wrath broke forth at the sight of his son, and he placed him in the sky with his sweetheart, where they now dwell, telling the sons and daughters of man to be obedient.' "

CHAPTER XVII

The wonders of the course of nature have ever challenged human attention. In savagery, in barbarism, and in civilization alike, the mind of man has sought the explanation of things. The Indians around Puget Sound have not been less curious than the other races. Like the rest, they have a strong yearning to understand the causes of all natural phenomena, such as the movement of the heavenly bodies, the change of the seasons, the succession of the night and day, the powers of air and water, the growth of trees, the overflowing of rivers, the curious forms of storm-carved rocks, the mysteries of life and death, the origin of the institutions of society all demand explanation. While the desire of the savage to know is as strong as it is with the civilized man, his curiosity is much more easily satisfied. The sense of the savage is dull compared with that of the civilized man: some people think that the barbarian has highly developed perceptive faculties. Nothing could be farther from the truth. For he sees few sights, hears few sounds, tastes of but few flavors, smells of but few odors, so by reason of the extreme narrowness of his experiences his whole sensible organization is coarse and blunt and his powers of penetration are limited. He experiences some things difficult to account for with his crude understanding. But he attempts to explain it nevertheless. To his understanding supernatural power is necessary to the performance of the acts which he describes, so he invents a story which explains the phenomena to his satisfaction. He repeats it to others and in their hands it grows and changes, becoming more refined and reasonable as the race advances. Thus are the mythologies, the philosophies, the religions, and the explanations of natural phenomena of the savage man evolved; and just in proportion as he advances in the scale of civilization the less he believes in these old traditions; the more difficult the phenomena of nature for him to explain, the more skeptical he becomes; in short, the more he knows, the less he thinks he knows.

Their folklore explains all of the phenomena of nature to the satisfaction of the savage, however foolish and simple it may seem to us.

Our Indians have not advanced far enough yet for their myths to contain any of those lofty ideals and refined sentiments which crept into the poetic legends of Greece, neither have they any conception of infinite power. But nevertheless the performances of their Demi-gods, with that queer mixture of power and weakness, and our "stick-siwashes" bear a striking resemblance. The myths of the origin of the world and of man, the fire-stealing, the romantic adventures of gods and heroes, and of the sun and moon, have much in common, one with the other.

The most remarkable character in lore of the Puget Sound Indian was old S'Beow. As the stories go, he is supposed to have been originally an Arctic or white fox; but changed himself into a man. Ki-ki, or the bluejay, was his grandmother. He had great power over his enemies although he was often misled and even killed by them. He could change himself into the form of any animal or thing he wished to; could cut himself to pieces and put himself together again, and do many other wonderful things. He is described as having cut himself in pieces and poking the pieces out through a small hole in an ice house in which he had been imprisoned and securing his liberty. There is also a story of S'Beow playing ball with his own eyes.

Eldridge Morse, who has atudied these legends systematically describes the Indians' conception of S'Beow as follows: He was a very short, pussy, big-bellied man who looked a little like Santa Claus, with a long, heavy white beard reaching to his waist; short white hair, sharp black eyes, sharp pointed ears like those of an Arctic fox, and small hands and feet. From either side of his mouth protruded an ugly cougar's tusk. He wore a short coat of mountain goat's wool and had four live bluejays for buttons.

An old Indian up on the Stillaguamish river believes that his father saw S'Beow once. He relates the experience as follows: At the southern point of Camano island there is an old land slide.

Many years ago there was a band of Indians camped at that point on the beach. His father and family were in a canoe paddling toward the camp. It was just dusk and the ruby rays of a summer sun-set had not yet disappeared. As if by magic or ta-mahn-a-wis, a man stood out on the bluff above them. He swelled himself up and again he swelled himself up until he was recognized as the form of old S'Beow, standing there as tall as the big fir trees. Presently S'Beow kicked the bluff over onto the Indians camped on the beach and buried them all, then stepped across onto Hat island and disappeared.

Indians riding by the spot mourn and wail and cry for them to this day. This fact together with the existence of the old slide at that place proves the truth of the whole story to the entire satisfaction of the savage.

It is very difficult to gather legends from the Puget Sound Indians, however. Rev. Myron Eels, the venerable missionary of the Skokomish reservation, Judge James G. Swan of Port Townsend, and Eldridge Morse, of Snohomish, have met with some success. The latter gentleman is the only one who has gathered them systematically and he has published nothing.

The Indians manifest much embarrassment when approached by a collector of traditions until they learn that he is already familiar with them, then his sailing is clear if he does not make fun of them. After all the investigator is not sure at the present day how much of the story is an Indian tradition and how much of it has been mixed with a story that some missionary has told.

CHAPTER XVIII

THE DEMON SKANA

The Makahs of Cape Flattery tell many stories of animals quite allegorical in their nature, which differ in details only from the legends of the other West coast tribes. One of their leading characters is the demon Skana. According to the Indian belief he can change himself into any form. There are many stories told of him. A long time ago the Indians were seal hunting in calm weather on a smooth sea. A killer whale kept close to the canoe, and the Indians amused themselves by throwing stones from their canoe ballast at him. The creature, tiring of this treatment, made for the shore, where it grounded on the beach. The curious Indians were attracted by a smoke which they saw curling up from the beach, and put for shore that they might learn its cause. Upon reaching the shore they were much surprised to find a large canoe, instead of Skana, on the beach, and that a man was on shore cooking some food by an out-door fire. He asked them why they threw stones at his canoe. "You have broken it," said he; "now go into the woods and get some cedar to mend it with."

After they had complied with his request he said to them: "Turn your backs to the water and cover your heads with your skin blankets, and don't look till I call you." They obeyed, and heard the canoe grate on the beach as it was being hauled into the surf. Then the man exclaimed: "Look now!" They looked and saw the canoe just going over the first breaker, the man sitting in the stern. They looked again and the canoe came up outside of the second breaker a killer, and not a canoe, with the man, or demon, in its belly. According to James G. Swain this allegory is common to all the tribes of the Northwest coast, and even in the interior where the salmon takes the place of the ocra, which never ascends fresh water rivers. To the north the Chilkat and other tribes carve the figure of a salmon, inside of which is the full length figure of a nude Indian.

A casual observer might mistake this for another Jonah story taught the Indians by the missionaries, but it is said to too far antedate their arrival.

James G. Swan tells the story of one legend of the man in the moon, which is common to the West coast Indians, and quite interesting.

The moon discovered a man about to dip his bucket into a brook after some water, so it sent down its arms, or rays, and grabbed the man, who, to save himself, seized hold of a big salal bush, but the moon being more powerful took the man, bucket and bush up to himself, where they have ever since lived, and can be seen every full moon during clear weather. The man is a friend of the wind god, and at the proper signal empties his bucket, causing it to rain on the earth.

CHAPTER XIX

Not far from the Snoqualmie hop ranch, on the Snoqualmie prairie, is a large mountain called Old Si, with what seems to be the image of a human form on the face of it. The story of its origin as told by the old Snoqualmie Indians, is one of the best legends that the Puget Sound Indians possess.

Snoqualm, the moon, then the king of the heavens, commanded the spider ty-ee (chief) to make a rope of cedar bark and stretch it from the sky to the earth. Upon seeing this, S'Beow's son, Si 'Beow, told Ki-ki, the bluejay, S'Beow's grandmother, to go up along the rope and then told his father to follow her.

The bluejay kept going up and going up and going up and S'Beow following after her, kept climbing up and climbing up and climbing up and the bluejay kept flying up and flying up and flying up a long time until she reached the under side of the sky, and S'Beow kept climbing up and climbing a-lo-ong time until he too got to where the great rope was fastened on the under side of the sky. And the bluejay began pecking away and she continued picking away and picking away and picking away until she made a hole through into the sky. It was well into the night when Ki-ki finished making her hole through and S'Beow followed after her into the sky. When S'Beow got through the hole he found himself changed himself into a beaver and got caught in a dead-fall beaver trap, which had been set by Snoqualm and when Snoqualm examined his trap in the morning he found a dead beaver with his skull crushed in. The Great Ty-ee took the beaver out of the trap, took the beaver to his home, skinned it, stretched the skin upon a hoop, hung it up to dry and threw the carcass over in the corner of his smoke house. All day long and well into the night S'Beow lay there, a dead beaver's carcass. At last Snoqualm fell into deep sleep and was heard snoring loudly. Then S'Beow got up, took his skin from the wall, removed it from the hoop and put it on himself and set about to explore the house of the Great Ty-ee. Outside the house he found some great forests of fir and cedar trees, which he pulled out by he roots and by his ta-mahn-a-wis (magic) made them small enough so that he could carry them under his arm.

He then entered the house and found hidden on one shelf the machinery that made the daylight, which he carried under the other arm. He took some fire from under the smoke hole, put some ashes around it and wrapped it with bark and leaves and carried it in one hand, in the other he carried the sun which he found hidden on the same shelf as the machinery which made the daylight. With all these things he proceeded to the lake out of which he had been trapped on the previous day, transformed himself into a beaver again, dove to the bottom of the lake and found where the spider Ty-ee had made the rope fast. He changed himself back into old S'Beow again and descended to earth, where he set out all the great trees around Puget Sound. He gave fire to the people, set the Sun in position and put the machinery that makes the daylight to working.

When Snoqualm awoke and saw what had been stolen, he in great rage pursued old S'Beow, going straight away to the place where the rope was made fast and started to descend to earth. The rope gave way with him and Snoqualm and the great rope fell in a heap making that great mountain near the head waters of the Snoqualmie river, and the outline of the human face which the Indian fancies to this day that he can see in the distance is what is left of old Snoqualm, once the Great King of the Heavens.

CHAPTER XX

One of the most common legends among the Indians around Puget Sound is the story of the stick-pan or the magic pan. "Stick-pan" is the Chinook name of a shallow wooden tray upon which the Puget Sound Indians served their food in their days of savagry. The story of the magic stick-pan was current among all the tribes of the region, each of them representing the scene of action to be along the river or stream most frequented by them.

According to their idea, S'Beow, although possessed of many supernatural powers, was thoroughly human. He could be led astray, overcome by superior force, killed or otherwise disposed of as easy as any other Siwash so far as his carnal self was concerned; but his spirit was unconquerable. The spirit was immortal and S'Beow was never so dangerous as just after he had been killed.

In defending the blind woman Skotah, S'Beow was overcome by superior force, killed and thrown into the river. All night his dead body drifted down the river. On the following day as he was rounding a bend in the stream he came in sight of some thin, pale blue smoke curling heavenward from a smouldering vine maple fire and on the bank of the river in front of it he beheld two squaws who were preparing a couple of silver salmon for their dinner.

By this time S'Beow's dead body had grown very hungry, even more hungry than he had ever been when alive, and he was at a loss to know how he could get something to eat. After a moment's reflection, however, a plan suggested itself; S'Beow transfomed himself into a very elegant, richly painted stick-pan. Immediately upon catching sight of it the squaws put out in the middle of the river in their canims (canoes) to catch it as it passed by.

"What a fine stick-pan," exclaimed one of the klootchmen.

"Just what we need," replied the other, or as the old Indians express it: "Ya-ka de-late klosh stick-pan," while the other replied : "Mi si-ka hi-as tick-kee o-coke."

They picked it up, put it in their canoe and paddled ashore. Upon reaching the spit they proceeded with the preparation of their dinner, resting their fish before the fire on crossed sticks and roasting it in Indian style.

They ate from their newly found stick-pan. While they were consuming the upper half of the first salmon the lower half disappeared, they knew not where. S'Beow had eaten it.

With a second salmon they met with a like experience for S'Beow was very hungry. At supper their previous experience was repeated, so thinking the stick-pan was possessed of demons and being very angry at it for consuming so much of their food, they smashed it to pieces.

At this stage old S'Beow cried with the voice of an infant: "I'll be your baby, I'll be your baby, if you dont hurt me."

S'Beow became their baby, was taken to their rancheree and placed on a board, a weight placed on his head and suspended from posts by two strings so that he might swing as in a hammock instead of being rocked in a cradle.

S'Beow was a "de-late klosh ten-as" (a very good baby). When the women were at home he would do much loving and cooing, but would rarely or never cry, but when they went out fishing or gathering salmon berries he would transform himself into old S'Beow, get up and eat of their stores of dried salmon until his enormous appetite was satisfied and would then change himself back into a baby again before the women returned.

Badly as these childless, lonely women wanted a baby, they could not help thinking that the baby was possessed of evil spirits and that he ate the dried fish either when they were absent from the house or when they were asleep.

At length they reached the conclusion that the baby was old S'Beow, and one night while the fire was yet burning they talked the matter over and resolved to kill him.

S'Beow, hearing this, again took upon himself the real character of S'Beow and departed. At dawn he reached the fish-trap where the women had caught their salmon and trout. He found it full of fish. His heart was aching for revenge so he destroyed the dam and allowed the fish to escape.

The fish were all very grateful to him for his kindness and they remembered him for it, so as he proceeded down the river the salmon and trout came and poked their heads out of the water at every meal time so that S'Beow could choose from among them the fish that he wanted to eat.

There seems to be niether moral nor location to this fragment of legend, but it illustrates clearly some features of old S'Beow's character as the average Puget Sound Indian used to understand him.

CHAPTER XXI

THE MAGIC BLANKET

One of the best stories known to the Indians around Puget Sound is the legend of the Ta-mahn-a-wis, or magic blanket.

Once upon a time there lived a boy with his parents on the shores of Puget Sound, who was just budding into young manhood. He had reached that point in life where boys prepare to fight life's battles for themselves, and where the Indians in former times sought to discover their totem, or guardian spirit. This boy went alone with his bow and arrow into the woods to hunt the little birds and little squirrels, and had good success in killing the little birds and little squirrels. He took the skins of the little squirrels and the feathers of the little birds and wove them into a blanket. Many days this little boy hunted in the woods for bird feathers and squirrel skins with which to make his blanket, until his parents, friends and all the rest of the people became suspicious of him and began to think that he was possessed of evil spirits.

Still the boy continued to work on his blanket day after day, from early dawn until nightfall, and all the while his friends knew not what he was doing. At length they became so much alarmed at the evil spirits of this young man that they picked up all their effects, and got in their canoes and sailed a long way across the waters, and left the boy alone in the woods without fire, food or shelter.

The boy went home at night after having completed his blanket, upon which he had been at work so long. When he found the home deserted he exclaimed, according to the rendering in classic Chinook:

"Halo piah, pe halo muck-a-muck, pe halo stick, pe halo ictas, pe halo tillicums. Nika de-late sick-tum·tum."

If he had spoken in English he would have said:

"There is no fire, and no food, and no house, and no pots, pans, kettles, no friends ; in short, nothing. It makes me sick at heart." He looked all round for his people, but could find no trace of them. They had taken all of the canoes with them so that he could not follow them. He then thought of his blanket. He went and got it and walked down the beach to the edge of the salt water. He dipped one corner of the blanket in the salt "chuck" and shook it, and out fell wood, and he shook it again and there was fire. Again he dipped the blanket in the water, and when he shook it out there were many little Siwashes to keep him company, and shaking it again, they became big Siwashes. Again he dipped his blanket in the water and shook it, and there were thousands of beautiful smelt. Just then a big bird came along and gobbled up all of the fish that it could carry and flew a long way over the waters with them to where the boy's people had gone.

The boy's old mother was on the beach looking across the waters and bewailing his sad fate, and thinking how she loved him and how sorry she was that she had left him, and how she wished she had not left him to perish there alone.

She thought she would see the rest of the people and see if she could not prevail on them to go back to her son, for she could not believe that he was possessed of demons. The woman looked up and saw a great bird flying from the direction where her boy was living. The bird flew directly into her canoe and began to spew up smelt. Between the pumping Kuhl-kulli, for that was the bird's name, would exclaim: "I-bro-ught-these-from-your boy ! I-bro-ught-these-from-your-boy !" The great bird continued to spew up fish until the canoe was half filled with smelt, all the while saying: " I brought these from your boy !" As the mother looked across the waters in the direction in which the bird came her heart leaped high with joy, for in the dim distance she beheld a smoke rising heavenward, which informed her that her boy was all right, for she knew that her boy could not starve with so many fish·and a fire to cook them. She was sure that he was possessed of a good, and not an evil, spirit.

The mother told her friends all about what had happened, and persuaded them to go with her back to where her son was living, and the boy and his parents, his old friends and his new friends all lived happily together for many years afterwards.

CHAPTER XXII

James Henry, a well known Indian of Port Gamble, who follows the sealing business is responsible for the story of the sky falling down.

A long time ago all the Indians with flattened heads lived away up north in the region of perpetual ice and snow. The parents of the race were ten brothers and all of them were very big men. They lived on deer and bear meat and the flesh of tarmigan or white grouse. They were all excellent archers and they killed so many white grouse with their bows and arrows that the Sagh-a-lie Tyee began to think that they would exterminate the species and he told them to kill no more white grouse for one "snow," or winter sea-son. They heeded him not, for they kept on slaughtering the grouse and eating them. In those days the sun passed over the earth from east to west and retraced its steps while they slept, and the sky was above the sun. One day the Sagh-a-lie Tyee became much angered at them for killing so many grouse, so he let the sky fall on them.

Then there followed a long hard winter and many people perished of hunger and cold for they had not killed bear and deer and prepared for the winter and it was so dark and there was so much ice and snow that they could not see to hunt and fish. These ten brothers awaited the return of day for a long time and at last the youngest of them in utter despair set about it and tried to lift up the sky with poles, and all his brothers helped him. They worked in this way for many months. They would raise one corner of the sky up so they could just see the day light and it would fall back on them, and again all would be total darkness, and all the land would be covered with ice and snow. At length, however, they got one big tall pole and all the Indians went to work with it and tried to prop the sky up, but for a long time they met with failure. At last, however, they succeed in getting the sky to start up long enough so that the sun could get under the great hollow hemisphere which they believe the sky to be, then the sun followed around the longest way in the day time of summer going back on the upper, or outside of the sky in the shortest route by night. In the winter months it passes across the under side of the sky by the shortest route, and back on the outside by the longest route so that ever since that time the Indians have had the longest days and shortest nights in the dry months of summer when they wanted to fish and hunt. It has always been light in the day time so that people could see to work, and dark at night so that they could sleep better, and the Indians have had the longest nights and shortest days in the wet months of winter when they could do but little and wanted to sleep most of the time.

CHAPTER XXIII

The story of the big flood is common to all the tribes around Puget Sound. The mountain referred to is usually the loftiest mountain nearest them. The Lummi Indians refer to Mt. Baker, the upper Stillaguamish to Mt. Pilchuck and the Nisquallies to Mt. Rainier, and each of them call their mountain Ta-ho-ma, from which is derived the name Tacoma. Ta-ho-ma means a lofty mountain, but does not refer to any peak in particular.

It was a long time ago, just after the breaking up of the great winter, that the sky opened and a terrible rain and snow deluged the world and the water kept on rising higher and higher until the great mountains were covered beneath it and ice and snow, and the bones of bear and deer and clam shells and fishbacks and logs floated on top of the water and settled on the mountain tops as the flood subsided. That is why the mountains are always covered with ice and snow. This also accounts for the presence of logs upon the tops of the mountains where trees have not grown and fish bones and clam shells and the like may be seen where they could not now exist.

Another legend of similar nature but more appropriately giving the Indian tradition of the first man and woman is told by one writer as follows :

There once fell upon the earth a long terrible rain ; the Whulge arose ; it filled the mountain walls, and all the tribes perished except one man. He fled before the rising waters up the sides of Mt. Rainier. The waters rose and covered the mountain. They swept over his feet ; they came to his knees, to his waist. He seemed about to be swept away, when his feet turned to stone.

Then the rain ceased. The clouds broke and the blue sky came again, and the waters began to sink.

The one man stood there on top of Rainier. He could not lift his feet ; they were rocks. Birds flew again, flowers bloomed again, but he could not go.

The Spirit of All Things came to him. "Sleep," said he. And the one man with stone feet slept.

As he slept there the Spirit of All Things took from him a rib and made of it a woman. When he awoke there stood his wife ready-made on the top of Mt. Rainier. His stone shoes dropped off and the happy pair came down the mountain to the wooded paradises of the Whulge on the sunset sea. Here sprung the human race at the foot of Rainier.

CHAPTER XXIV

ORIGIN OF SUN AND MOON

Joe Anderson, a Port Madison Indian, tells the story of the origin of the sun and moon, a story which many of the Indians still continue to believe, notwithstanding their present Christian education.

Long, long ago an Indian woman went to a creek to wash some clothes and left her little babe at home alone. When she returned she found that the child had been stolen and she wept bitterly. When she again went to the creek to wash she took the baby's clothes with her. While washing, some of the baby's dresses sunk to the bottom of the creek and some mud got on the inside of them. When she lifted them out of the water the mud was transformed into another baby. However, it was not a bright clean baby like the other, but a very black and dirty one. The new baby thrived and grew very rapidly and the mother loved it dearly, although she longed for her kidnapped child to return.

When the new baby got big enough he was always out at play in the mud puddles, seldom returning until late at night.

After awhile the prodigal boy returned and played with the other boy, who still continued to wear a dirty face.

The parents loved the clean boy best and the dirty boy became very jealous. So one day the dirty boy thought he would go home as clean as the other boy and spent the whole day in washing himself. At night when he returned he was as clean and bright as the sun, and his brother who had hitherto been so clean shone only like the moon in comparison. Then the clean boy said : " You be the sun and I'll be the moon," and together they flew away and the once dirty boy became the spirit of the sun which throws bright light on the earth by day, and the once lost boy became the moon which reflects dim light on the earth by night.

MASK USED TO APPEASE CRYING CHIL-
DREN—OLD-MAN-HOUSE TRIBE

CHAPTER XXV

SKOBIA THE SKUNK

Quite an interesting legend is the one describing how Skobia the Skunk came to be so small as he is :

A long time ago there lived a pole-cat who was the parent of all the race of skunks. He was a great skunk. In size he approached the cinnamon bear ; his perfume was strong in proportion, while his tread was correspondingly heavy and loud. Many were the nightly visits of "Skobia," as the skunk is called by the Indian, to their camps and great was the damage to life and comfort caused by him.

The Indians were at a loss to know what to do with Skobia, but at length they thought of old S'Beow and sent for him. Upon his arrival on the scene S'Beow caused them all to get in a great potlatch house, a large building used by the Indians of the Northwest coast on their ceremonial occasions. Then they all set themselves to cutting a big pile of vine maple wood and bringing it into the potlatch house. At length when a sufficient pile of wood had been gathered together they built a great and very hot fire of the wood. They fastened up all the doors and each Indian cut himself a cudgel about six feet long. All but old S'Beow went to bed and pretended to be asleep.

Along about midnight, after the fire had burned to a bed of live coals the heavy tread of Skobia was heard approaching the potlatch house. To illustrate the heavy tread of Skobia, the Indian will get down on all fours and slap the palm of his hands heavily on the ground after the fashion of the bear, skunk, weasel and other flat-footed quadrupeds.

CHARM MASK AGAINST THE EVIL EYE—OLD-MAN-HOUSE TRIBE

Skobia came to the door and demanded admittance, but no one paid any attention to him. He then begged of them and plead with them and told them that he was their friend and wanted to come in to see them. At length old S'Beow pretended to rouse up and, like one just waking from a deep sleep, he stretched and yawned and inquired of Skobia what he wanted. '' I am your friend and I want to come in and visit you,'' replied Skobia. '' You'r a skunk and will stink us out ! '' said old S'Beow. '' I'm your friend ! I won't hurt you,'' replied Skobia. At last S'Beow told Skobia how he might enter the house. Skobia was advised to go up on the roof, blindfold himself and just reach his toes down through the opening in the smoke hole so that S'Beow could catch hold of them. He did so and S'Beow caught hold of them and quickly opened up the smoke hole and threw Skobia down on the bed of burning coals.

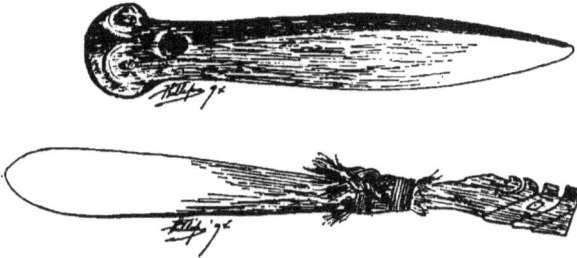

STONE AND COPPER WAR CLUBS—TAKEN FROM SKOKOMISH INDIANS

The Indians then who pretended to have been asleep all this time, but who had not been asleep at all, sprung to their feet, grabbed their cudgels and turned Skobia over and over on the live coals and they kept turning him over, and turning him over, and Skobia kept growing smaller, and growing smaller, a long time until he was no larger than a rat and would not stink enough to hurt anybody. They then opened the door, kicked him out and ever since then the skunk has been a very small animal and no Indian has been afraid of him.

CHAPTER XXVI

Of the Shilshohs, a tribe once inhabiting the country about Salmon bay and in ante-civilized times all the country from Smith's cove and Lake Union north to the Snohomish river, there is not at this time a single known representative living, the tribe is extinct. Of these Indians little is known. Dr. H. A. Smith, of Smith's cove, who settled among them about the time of the first settlement of Seattle, probably has the best general knowledge of these bygone people. He furnished the author the following particulars :

When I settled here in 1853 about a dozen Indian families of the Shilshoh tribe were still living on Salmon bay and I learned from them that within the recollection of their old men they numbered between 500 and 600 including children, and according to tradition their numbers once ran up into the thousands and that they occupied the entire country from Smith's cove and Lake Union to the Snohomish river. They claimed that the cause of their rapid decline was owing to frequent raids made upon them by the Northern or Stickeen Indians, who visited the Sound every year for the purpose of plunder ; that they were a very cruel people who delighted in murder and never spared prisoners except for the purpose of enslaving them. That they lived in constant dread of their northern and warlike foes is evident from a circumstance that came under my own observation in the fall of 1853.

Desiring to reload a revolver that had become somewhat rusty, I stepped out into the yard and fired five or six shots in rapid succession about 8 o'clock in the evening.

Three days after one of the Shilshohs came to my house in a very agitated frame of mind to inquire if I had seen anything of the Stickeens. He said his folks heard rapid firing in the direction of my house three nights before and thought I had been attacked by the Northern Indians, perhaps killed, and, to save themselves his people had all taken to the woods, where they were still in hiding. He had skulked around by Lake Union and along near Salmon bay and up to my house to learn if possible whether the Stickeens had left Salmon bay. Although I assured him that I had been the innocent cause of their alarm it was several days before they ventured back.

The few families that were here when I first came to live in the Cove melted away like a morning frost. Gambling is a ruling passion among nearly all Indians and I attribute their rapid extinction largely to that vice.

After the "Bostons," as they called Americans to distinguish them from the Hudsons bay traders, came among them they soon began to live better. They bought flour, beans, rice, clothes, blankets, and many of the more enterprising among them lived quite comfortably until a gambling mania would seize them when they would frequently gamble off everything they owned, even their clothes, and then sleep on the bare ground or some newly gathered ferns or moss and so nearly naked. The result of course would be colds ending in pneumonia or consumption.

Dr. Jim, a genuine herb doctor, who was quite renowned for his many astonishing cures among the sable sons of the forest, was the last of the Shilshohs. He was really a superior Siwash, manly, fine looking and intelligent, and during the last years of his chequred life he spoke the English language fluently. About fifteen years ago he grew weary of this world and left it by hanging himself to a rafter in his own house at the mouth of the Shilshoh bay one morning while his old wife was preparing breakfast.

Never having been blessed with offspring and his last wife being a lake Indian, his death struggles ended the cares of a man-cursed tribe, once famed for its manly men and comely maidens. Of course they were not comely viewed from the standpoint of a cultured American esthete, but the maidens with fine features and red cheeks were as beautiful to the tawny hunter tribes as a Hebe would be to a Bostonian.

Of their life and legends Dr. Smith never fully acquainted himself. Here is one tribe of native people at least who will pass into oblivion with scarcely a line left to the history-loving and history-writing people who have taken their places. One legend alone and that the pioneer has reduced to verse has been preserved. The legend, as it appears, was written 40 years ago merely for the pleasure of it by the old pioneer and never was offered for publication. It is tinged with romance and relates to an Indian maiden whose betrothed was killed during a raid by the Northern or Stickeen Indians to Shilshoh bay. The Indian maiden's grief was so great that she became deranged and on several occasions started alone in search of the absent lover in a canoe imagining she could sail to the happy hunting grounds and into the sunshine of his happy presence. One morning she was missing and as her lover's canoe was gone and as her tracks proved that she had taken it her friends easily guessed her fate :

GAZELLE, THE FOREST MAIDEN.

The birds and the beasts had retired to rest,
    The sun's lingering rays from the mountains had fled,
And angels had folded away from the west
    The wind-woven curtains of purple and red.

The moon's silver morning had mantled the hills,
    Inviting the world's weary millions to lay
Their sorrows aside for the beauty that thrills
    And soothes into silence the cares of the day.

When, lured by the luster of mountain and lea,
    A maniac-maiden stole out of her tent
To wander and weep by the sorrowing sea
    And sadden the night with her mournful lament.

A sibylline song to her lover she sang,
    As she sat in the moonlight alone by his grave,
And a more mournful strain on the night never rang
    Or saddened the soul of a guardian brave.

" How oft have I seen him when only a child,
    His forehead with feathery fetishes crownded,
Arrest with his arrow the deer in the wild,
    Or bring the gray swan from the sky to the ground.

" How oft have I seen a strange light in his eyes
    As over the white foaming billows we whirled
And watched the red lightnings dart down from the skies
    To pilot the hurricane over the world.

" No more by the tempest tossed sea will he stroll,
    No more will he worship the wilderness here,
For his spirit has gone to the home of the soul
    Where bison and elk are abundant as deer.

" O that the Great Spirit would answer my plea
    And bear me away on the wings of the waves
To that lovlier land that lies over the sea,
    Where winds never moan over moss-covered graves."

While singing, her eyes by fatality strayed
    To a little canoe, that she loved as her life,
In which they had sailed from a flowery glade
    The morning he promised to make her his wife.

Soon a wild fancy seized her, she paused not to ask
  A moment its meaning, her only desire
Was strength to perform the congenial task
  Her *genius loci* saw fit to inspire.

A brief minute more and the bark was untied,
  With a fluttering heart and a tremulous hand,
And launched on the waters, so lonely and wide,
  That rapidly hurried away from the land.

" I'll find him ! I'll find him ! " she shouted in glee,
  " His tent must be pitched in some flowery dell
In the land of the sachems beyond the blue sea
  Where now he is waiting to welcome Gazelle."

The full moon was nearing the noonday of night,
  The waves sang the songs she had loved when a child,
And her young, happy heart was elate with delight
  As they bore her away from her dear native wild.

And as onward she sped at the tide's rapid pace,
  Alone with her heart and the heavens above,
The silent stars looked on her young, sinless face,
  Too full of faith's pathos, with pity and love.

For, far to the westward the winds were at war,
  And soon sudden darkness spread over the world,
The waves were abroad with a hoarse, sullen roar
  And nearer and colder they eddied and curled.

The moon and the stars with their stillness were gone,
  Red meteors darted anon through the dark,
And fate seemed to hurry the hurricane on
  Where rocked on the billows a rudderless bark.

When Neptune, near morning, the billows had bound
  And stars hung in heaven like spangles of gold,
Deep down in the regions of silence profound
  A form, faintly human, lay lifeless and cold.

But where, oh ye winds, is the maniac-maiden ?
  And what of love's hopes that so often have lied ?
Let us trust she arrived at the red hunter's Aiden
  And greeted the warrior awaiting his bride.

CHAPTER XXVII

Beyond the black range of the Olympic mountains, which can be seen stand-ing out in such bold relief against the western horizon from the bluffs about the cities of the Sound on bright days, sits the little village of the Quinaiult Indians, whose last remnant of a once mighty tribe now scarce numbers a hundred persons. There's a long shingle of beach, a glistening reach of sand, bright under the glare of summer suns, with a broad sweep of salty bay, flecked here and there with a few jagged and black-looking rocks, the sporting ground of the sea otter the year round. Outside the line of pointed rocks the swells from the restless Pacific ocean come tumbling in and are broken into white foam and dashing spray upon the rocks or, missing those roll on upon the beach and curl the shimmering reach of sand into pretty riffles. At the rear is a dense background of forest that reaches far into the interior until it runs out at the timber line far up the sloping sides of the Olympics. The Quinaiult river rushes out through the tangle of forest past the village and pours its purling waters into the long stretch of bay, as if glad to escape from the imprisonment of woods and jungle. The little village is an ideal scene, one to swell the ambitions of the artist, and to please the fancy of the legend-lover or the story teller. To the north'ard many miles and on clear days can be seen the jutting outline of Cape Flattery, that most northwesterly point of land in these United States, and around whose base the waters of the ocean surge and roll and never rest, and where, 'tis said, " a day has never passed whereon it has not rained."

To the south'ard is the long reach of coast land, with few breaks, that runs away into the distant perspective and finally loses itself in a hazy and blue horizon. Many, many moons ago, so runs the tradition of the Quinaiults, their people were numbered by the thousands, and they held a great power over other and adjacent tribes, above that of any tribe that inhabited all the coast lands thereabouts. But many changes have taken place since the sun of the ancient Quinaiult was in the zenith. The warriors of the tribe lie buried in the dense copse and wood that feather-edge the great sand stretches of the ocean beach, and a degenerated handful of men and women and children, a few dogs and chickens keep watch over the graves and cling to the little grass plats that formed the neucleus of their once almost boundless domain. Worse far, all their happy hunting grounds have been curtailed by a maternal government until now but a stretch of ocean beach and a narrow breadth of mighty forest land is all that is left that they can call their own.

One street, crooked in a right angle half way in its length, serves the little village for a thoroughfare, aye, more than answers, for little use have the handful of Quinaiults who are left for street or thoroughfare other than the naked beach. The ocean shore is their highway and the cedar canoe their favored and their only equipage, and they ask for nothing better.

Of their habitations there is not much to attract except in their very quaintness. There are very few and as the years roll by there will be fewer still, for the Quinaiults will soon be known only in history or musty tradition. Several of their rude structures, bare imitations copied from the whites who have crowded them down upon the narrow beach, are raised on stilts or elevated foundations just out of reach of the turbulent tides. These raised structures are not, however, the rule, for the larger number line the little foot-path out of reach of the restless waters. The majority of the buildings have for the floor the mother earth. The exteriors generally are as rude as the floor. An ordinary barn far outranks the unclassic habitation of the older Quinaiults, and even the rising generation fails in its efforts to approach the rudest ideal of the Boston man.

The "renaissance" erections of Quinaiult and also the two government buildings, for there is an agency on the ground, only serve to contrast with the ultra-conservatism apparent in the greater portion of this veritable wind-washed place. Hand-riven cedar, now darkly stained and moss-covered by age, rudely but snugly laid together after the fashion of a barn, describes the exterior. But within, what study! The colder comfort of the exterior has vanished. There is little light, for there are no windows, and the smoke from the fire which burns somewhere within hides one's view. Gradually, however, one can see.

The household is generally squatting upon rush mats, with darkened faces and queer fashion presenting a strange picture illumined by the glow of the small log fire. The most conspicuous of the group, perhaps, will be an old woman or older man of short stature and appearing broken down with age. The rank growth of heavy gray hair, for all wear it to its full length, covers almost entirely the small, wizened features, now characteristic of little but decrepitude and imbecility, but showing a sharply receding forehead, sharp eyes, and small, regular teeth, yet preserved with fair whiteness; covered with a parti-colored shawl or blanket, clothed in an ordinary skirt and bodice, or with a dirty, faded shirt, if it be a man, and decorated with ancient trinkets which have dangled from the ears for perhaps a hundred years, forms one only of the old dames or graybeards who are found attached to the Quinaiult household. If a squaw, her time is occupied stirring the contents of an iron kettle containing salmon, while other members of the family engage in mat-making or basket-weaving. One or two 'fat and naked little Quinaiults are also in view, playing with the domestic pets of all kinds—chickens, cats and dogs. They are watched by the mother with a truly maternal care. The latter displays, with average height but heavy proportions, a healthy, active form, indicating a strength not much inferior to that of her liege lord and husky-looking husband. Indeed, the woman is built for the work in which she so exerts herself when poling in the canoe on the rapids of her own Quinaiult river, for a long reach of their favorite stream running back into the hills the tribe holds as part of its own domain. Her features are full and round, of the usual Flathead type, and display an intelligence immediately remarked in contrast with her aged kindred. Though living in huts no better than stables or outhouses, she is contented, rather neat in attire and not unhappy.

But the truer type of the tribe, the head of the household, is also there, a living study for the enthusiast—a portrait not yet portrayed. His face and his bearing recall the Indian stoic of romance and bring to mind the heroes of the sun dance. In youth this full-blooded nomad of the water had slain three men in single-handed combat or accomplished other warlike deeds. There is some trace of thought in his countenance, and, notwithstanding the flat head he bears himself as a freeman. The eye of the man is small and oblique, well lashed, and surmounted by heavy eyebrows. The nose is wide, not very prominent ; mouth large, and of impressive line. His figure is well balanced— a heavy frame covered by rounded flesh, not particulary sinewy. His negligee is a shirt only—there is no orthodox dress for the male portion of the tribe.

Types in the tribe are greatly varied at this late, or rather last, period of existence. The specific characteristic is the flat head.

In physique the Quinaiult cannot compare with his brother of the plains. He has matured in the damp shadows of the forest and in the cramped limits of the cedar canoe—not on the boundless prairie. The group before us, however, shows signs of health and strength, without great vivacity.

The method of dining is as simple as the meal itself, for each of the family dips promiscuously into a kettle with a small ladle of horn. Salmon, often without other addition whatever to the bill of fare, is relished to excess.

Since the days to which their earliest tradition extends the lordly salmon has graced the Quinaiult's frugal board. True the waters that wash up against his rude dwelling contain countless thousands of other fish, but they never show themselves in the fresh water streams.

Of game they have but little, and as the years go by what little they have been used to gradually diminishes. Salmon is the chief staple diet and will continue to be so until the last Quinaiult has departed to the happy fishing grounds.

Besides the salmon and other fish the older Quinaiults lived upon the products as well of the forest and the stream, as do in a measure the remnant of the tribe now left. Encroaching civilization has driven the game almost out of his reach now, for the Quinaiult is a hunter who doesn't like trailing through the dense woods. He must now depend on a relish from the garden of some sort to take the place of the juicy steaks of the game of the forest.

In the waters of the ocean they still seek the valuable sea otter, the seal, and sea lion, and at times the whale from which everything eatable almost is sent to the larder. In the woods they still track the deer, the elk and the bear and trap the otter, the beaver and the mink at the river brink, though had they still to depend upon these for sustenance they would go to bed on half rations. The furs they secure, however, go a good ways in keeping the proverbial wolf from the door of their hovels.

In the ocean and river chase, however, is where these redmen excel, for they have literally been bred, born and brought up on the waters. Bravery in the canoe, on the surf or in the rapid rivers where no other craft can live, is the leading virtue of the Quinaiult. He will pack in his ictas and his household, and course the waters of the river or the coast and send the canoe spinning through the strongest currents that chase about the base of Flattery Rocks with the daring hardihood of a Dohomian warrior in battle. He will course along the coastland in waters that no ordinary vessel will attempt and seldom is it that the Quinaiult population is decreased by wrecks at sea.

The Quinaiult has no excessive love of life. He is stoic, living in the hope of the happy hunting or fishing ground, and a few years ago the custom of slaying the pony of the dead at the grave was still practiced. It is even now the custom to place the gold of the dead in the mouth and hands, burying it with them. "They will need it on the journey to the happy hunting grounds," and the cupidity of the Quinaiult is never aroused at the sight of gold when one of his people dies, for they like all other western Indians have an excessive love of family.

Along the somber banks of the Quinaiult river at this day are many graves, bearing on the exterior, in decorative form, the minor personal belongings of the body within. There were graves pointed out which were made earlier than their tradition records and once graceful canoes of cedar placed above their dead owners are now crumbling into unshapely forms.

Marriage is a simple institution of "take a wife and live with her."

The potlatch dance, or gift feast, is the year's social event at Quinaiult.

Upon the acquirement of wealth the fortunate man issues a manifest to his own and other tribes that it is his intention to hold a potlatch merriment. He gives up his entire fortune, for he acquires thereafter the title of "tyee" or chief. Presents of all values are lavishly distributed to those who attend. It is a grotesque ceremony and lasts many days.

The superstition of the tribe forms a wierd chapter. The medicine man is the chief factor. He has in his possession hideously painted and carved wooden images, shamens of wonderful power in Quinaiult. Representing grossly exaggerated human proportions, and of no merit as a work of art, they bear no description. It is in sickness that these "big medicines," as they are called, are used by the doctor, who remains in practice against all devices of the evil one to suppress his power.

One of the latest affairs in which this big medicine was practiced, resulted in the death of three children, all of the same family, after many weeks of noisy demonstration by the doctors. The father's wealth was spent in heavy payments to the medicine men, called by him from various tribes to administer to his sick girls, who at first showed nothing more than the symptoms of a simple disease. In company with the doctors also were many neighbors, who crowded the limited quarters of the sick room to suffocation, in the performances of their wild orgies. Night and day would be heard the horse chant of the medicine men, chorused vociferously by the crowd, and the beating of the tom-tom drum. The young ones lay helpless and unattended, without hope or chance of recovery.

Few strangers pass through the village without hearing the noise of the tom-tom, and the chant of death at the sick bed. However trifling the complaint the medicine man is called and heavily recompensed for his services.

The indulgence of superstition, however, is better illustrated by the recent conduct of the unhappy mother of a child which became slightly sick. The incident happened during one of the cold and stormy nights of winter. Darkness had long announced the hour of sleep when a wailing cry was heard coming from the side of the river, where nothing but a forest-covered bluff exists. The cry was one almost of agony and was continued throughout the night. At times the wail of woe would be borne away by the soughing of the woods in the gale or be drowned by the roar of breakers close at hand. No light was seen. With the faith of a fanatic and endurance of a mother's love the mourner spent the night alone in the cold and rain, wrapped in no cover but a single blanket, in the belief that the evil spirit would not find her babe in the darkness. The strange faith of the woman is paralleled by the worship practiced by an old medicine man, still living, of the tribe. In a dilapidated dwelling the Indian erected a charred hemlock pole of slight dimensions, securing thereto a covering of eagle and other feathers. The idol was complete in its simplicity and exemplified a tradition of the medicine man's power. Its significance, however, remains buried within the bosom of the taciturn worshiper. For days and nights he knelt beside this strange design without eating, without sleeping, but partly chanting, partly talking, with earnest gesture and uplifted face, he called up the mystery of his superstition.

The great highway of the tribe, next to the ocean itself, is the swiftly flowing Quinaiult river, up which they run their light canoes to the lake of the same name. In the summer and sometimes, too, when the snow whitens the upper lying forests, the canoe highway is relinquished and the Indian takes the trail through the woods or over the mountains. From the lake of Quinaiult, resting in the foothills of the Olympics, within hearing of the ocean's roar, many trails are blazed to camps, made long years ago, where fat elk have been butchered and dried by the Indians.

The mountains form the summer's paradise of the tribe. It is there that bands of elk may be seen gamboling on the unmelted snow in the glare of the sun ; and the black bear may be seen in numbers feeding on the luxurious wild berries. But the lake itself, perhaps, is regarded by the Indians as their greatest natural treasure. The year round it is the haunt of numerous kinds of salmon, tempted there from the ocean to spawn. Thousands of trout may be seen also in its transparent depths and wild fowl flock to its inviting feeding grounds in great numbers from all climes. At times, too, a deer makes its way from bank to bank. It is an ideal spot, but will not much longer be the domain of the Quinaiult tribe.

The interior of the Quinaiult hut is more interesting than the outside. In the smoke and dull light the details of the house are almost invisible. The mountings of a rack of firearms, seven or eight in number, attract inquiry as they glimmer in the firelight. They are relics of many years with the exception of one or two. The most ancient is a flint-lock, of immense bore and short barrel, the stock being inlaid with native work of bone. Another is an old muzzle-loading Kentucky rifle standing as high as the hunter himself ; and of more recent date is the old reliable Sharp's, picked up by the present generation in their migrations to the hop fields on Puget Sound or in barter.

Here and there many things tell of the chase—the short thick string bow of Alaska cedar, together with a quiver of feathered arrows, steel traps and the salmon and otter spears (fir poles an inch in diameter and 18 feet long) mounted with two keen points of elk or deer horn, and secured by thongs of rawhide, and a dozen other curious relics. The domestic belongings of the family are within the building. Canoe poles of young hemlock and the strong, light and gracefully made paddles of native yew-wood are stowed away under the roof. Hanging on the walls are rush mats, clam baskets and more fancifully-designed baskets delicately weaved of dyed spruce roots, forming one of the more profitable pastimes of the women. Relics of the hunt, hides, furs, tanned skins, horns and skulls are in every odd corner. Fresh meats and fresh salmon are hung in the cool shade without the house. Salmon is also hung up to dry in the sun without, and masses of salmon are hanging from the rafters within, curing by smoke from the daily fires. Salmon aroma is everywhere.

There is no furniture proper. The. family beds are laid upon platforms raised a few inches from the floor, with a few rush mats for mattresses. The appearance of the whole interior is primitive to a degree. It is a study on nature's own farm.

Probably of all their pastimes the sea otter chase lends the greatest excitement and shows the Quinaiult Indian at his best. The otter loves the surf that tosses about around and over the jutting rocks that fringe a few islands out in the bay in front of the village. Strong tides rush in eddying currents between the rocks and the shore line, and following these the Quinaiult pushes his sea boat out on the leeward side of the rocks and meets the glossy-coated animal in his most pleasant haunt. The smoothbore is now used largely by the present hunters, but the spear once formed the only weapon used in the chase as the bow and quiver did on land.

The Quinaiult builds himself a lookout on shore and a sentinel is at all convenient times perched up aloft with his gaze seaward, on the lookout for any object of the chase by sea. When a whale or otter or a herd of seals is spied the sentinel gives the warning and all able-bodied members of the tribe rush for the fleet of canoes always drawn up on the beach.

Few ships appear in the offing and fewer steam vessels beat the waters along the shoreline, for Quinaiult is nearly midway between Gray's harbor and the entrance to the straits at Cape Flattery. There are no roads leading across country to the distant settlements on the Sound, and Quinaiult is therefore a lonesome place. The white settler is encroaching upon the Quinaiult, but his life must be largely an extension of the native's for many years to come until the friendly railroad reaches him—if it ever does.

QUINIAULTS HUNTING HAIR SEAL

CHAPTER XXVIII

TRADITION OF A GREAT INDIAN BATTLE

The Puget Sound Indians have a tradition of a great battle in which the Quillayutes were almost annihilated :

For many years in the early days of the country, as early as 1869, residents of what is now Jefferson county were puzzled over the vast number of human bones, principally skulls, that lay scattered about the beach not far from the military post that had been established at Port Townsend. That a great Indian battle had been fought and great slaughter made by the defeated, was plain but where and by whom was a mystery. The Indians then resident near the post were mysterious and non-committal on the subject and their chiefs smoked and were mute. The noted paper chief, Duke of York, though the heydey of his power was gone, was still an important personage among the Indians and settlers and from him Mr. J. A. Kuhn, then residing at Port Townsend, decided to obtain the information so much desired. Strategy alone could succeed ; mild persuasion had been tried often and by various ones. The great chief of the Clallam tribe persistently refused to tell and insisted vehemously that he could not account for the presence of the human relics. However, Mr. Kuhn one day induced the old chief to accompany him to an island in the Sound to search for shells, leaving the chief's two wives, Jenny and Queen, who were always his traveling companions, at home. While there, Mr. Kuhn after all endeavors to get the Indian to divulge the story of the battle had failed, told the chief to call at his home on a certain day and he would show him a sign from heaven and prove to the Indians that he was no ordinary

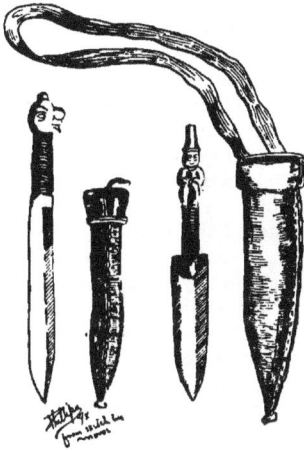

COPPER AND IRON DAGGERS, MOOSE HIDE SHEATH—SOUND INDIANS

being and that if the Duke did not tell him all he knew of the massacre he would cause the chief and his people great trouble. The noble old Indian with a large retinue of followers was on hand at Mr. Kuhn's house on the day appointed. Mr. Kuhn's trick was the old one of bringing on the darkness, and the untutored and savage mind was to be awed by an eclipse. The white man's power of foretelling being ascribed to the supernatural and a direct connection with the spirits that control all things on the earth and in the sky. It was known to Mr. Kuhn that on the day set for the appearance at his house of the old Indian there would be an eclipse of the sun sufficient in importance to overawe the mind of the chief and compel him to tell the story from fear. When the eclipse occurred the old chief readily complied and told the story of a great massacre of the people of the Quillayute tribe whose possessions extended along the Pacific ocean south of Cape Flattery and joining on the straits that of the Clallam tribe over which the old Duke reigned on the east.

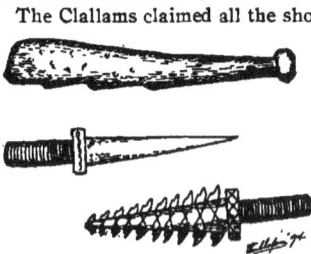

The Clallams claimed all the shore of the country extending from Pysht on the straits of Fuca to Hood's canal. The Quillayutes had invaded part of the ground claimed by the old Indian and his tribe. They hunted in their woods, fished for their salmon and dug their clams without permission. Hatred for them soon caused the Duke of York to plot their extermination. The Clallam tribe not being strong enough of themselves to make war upon the invaders, the

TWANA WAR CLUBS

crafty old chief sent emissaries to the Skagit tribe to induce them to enter with him upon a war. The mission was successful and a number of their allies prepared to commence the slaughter of the unsuspecting enemy. The Quillayutes at the time were encamped upon the beach fishing and merry-making all unconscious of the terrible fate so soon to overtake them. They were there with all their ictas, their papooses scampering about the white sands, or scudding through the woods in the rear while the death-dealing Duke of York was planning their destruction. The Skagit Indians brought on the attack by appearing in front of the peaceful Quillayute camp in canoes, yelling and hooting to attract the attention of the enemy and bring them all out and down to the beach. The old Duke of York and his warriors, who were hidden in the woods in the rear, rushed out of their hiding places and the slaughter began. The Skagit warriors landed and the battle was soon raging fiercely. The attacking parties were too strong and the Quillayutes were soon at their mercy. The battle lasted but a short time and soon there was not a Quillayute brave left. There is nothing to mark the site of the great slaughter at this day save a few ghastly skulls whose wide eyeless sockets stare up at the passerby from their bed of gravel on the beach. Picnics are now held on the old battle ground and it sometimes happens while some young lady and her lover stroll about the shaded paths, or seated on some mystic seat their tete-a-tete is interrupted by a sudden view of one of these mementoes of the once numerous tribe of Quillayutes.

Another account which seems to cover much the same similar occurrence at the same place gives it that the tribe of the Duke of York were massacred with the exception of a very few. This took place, so it is related, when the

A QUINIAULT HUT

old Duke was a small Indian about 14 years of age. The assailants were Sitkas, T'Klinkit or some other band of Alaska Indians who came by the way of Oak bay, near Ludlow, across the spit to the present site of Hadlock, caught the Clallams asleep and killed some 600 of them. It is claimed that the remains are still discoverable at that point. As the Duke was about 80 when he died some years ago, this must have taken place between 1820 and 1825.

The first raid affecting the white population of the Sound was when a crowd of T'Klinkits (or in this case probably some more southerly tribe) came to Whidby island in 1855 and murdered Colonel Ebey, then collector of customs for the Puget Sound district. They not only murdered him, but beheaded him. Several of his posterity are now living and can give full facts in this case.

CHAPTER XXIX

Sealth, second chief of the allied tribes in early days and previously of the Squamish and Duwamish, was the greatest Indian character of the country. Like the historic chief of the Mingoes, he was a friend of the white man and enemies he had none. A statesman and not a warrior he swayed the minds of his people with the magic of oratory rather than of war. Without a knowledge of the polyglot language common to all the tribes and the early white men, he was able by his superiority of mind to mould the turbulent and warlike spirits about him to his way of thinking, and to not only control them individually but to unite them into one grand peace union and to ever after maintain over them against all opposition a power as potent for good as the spirit and nature of the one who prompted it. Many chiefs who had before enjoyed chiefship without hinderance and directed and controlled his people at his own sweet will yielded to the superior power of Sealth, acted his part after the federation only as a lieutenant or sub-chief. Many old-timers yet survive who enjoyed the friendship of the old chief. Samuel F. Coombs, who probably has as intimate a knowledge of the early Indians as any one living, says of the old chief Sealth :

" The first time I ever saw Chief Sealth was in the summer of 1860, shortly after my arrival, at a council of chiefs in Seattle. At that time there was an unusually large number of Indians in town, over 1000 of them being congregated on the sandy beach. Most of the Indians were standing around talking in groups or listening to the deliberations of the council of about twenty of the oldest Indians seated in a circle on the ground. The chief figure was a venerable-looking old native, who was apparently acting as judge, as all who spoke addressed themselves to him. Matters of grave importance were evidently being discussed, and I was greatly impressed with the calm and dignified manner in which the old judge disposed of the matter in dispute and the great attention and respect shown him when speaking. From an intelligent-looking Indian who could speak English I learned that the old judge was Chief Seattle, or, as he was then known, Sealth, and that those seated about him were ex-chiefs and leading Indians of the various tribes then living about here.

Chief SEALTH

SEATTLE

J RAPHAEL COOMBS 93

Among them were Seattle Curley from the mouth of the Duwamish ; Tecumseh, from the Black river ; Shilshole Curley, from Salmon bay ; Lake John from Lake Washington, and Kitsap, from Kitsap county.

" With this young man as an interpreter I interviewed several of the oldest natives as to how Sealth became head chief of so many tribes. They said that about fifty years before that time, when Sealth was 20 or 22 years old, news reached the various tribes in this vicinity that a large number of the mountain or upper Green and White river Indians were preparing to make a raid upon the salt water tribes. Great anxiety was felt among the latter, as the mountain tribes were redoubtable warriors, and had on several previous occasions vanquished the salt water tribes and carried off many of their people as slaves. Accordingly a council of war, composed of the chiefs and leading warriors of the tribes expecting to be attacked, met at the Old-Man-House near Port Madison. This place was the principal rendesvous of these tribes for potlatches and councils. At this council many plans were discussed as to the best method of resisting the invaders. None of those suggested by the older men, however, was satisfactory, and then the younger men were called upon for suggestions. At length young Sealth, a member of the Old-Man-House tribe, presented his plan, and it was so well devised and so clearly presented, that without listening to any others, it was adopted and he was appointed to carry it out, being given command of the expedition.

" Information had reached the salt water tribes that a large force of the mountain tribes intended to come down the Green and White rivers in canoes and inaugurate their attack at night. Sealth organized a band of warriors, and the day before the raid was expected they went up the river to a place on White river, near where John Fountain now lives above Black river bridge, and where the bluff on one side reaches to the river edge. The river here makes a short bend, and the current is very swift. A little below the bend a large fir tree standing on the bank was felled in such a way that it reached across the river and lay only a few inches above the water, so that no canoe could go under without upsetting. The work of felling the tree was done with rude axes, some made of stone, and it took the band nearly the whole day to bring it down and get it into position, which was finally accomplished before sunset. Sealth then ambushed his warriors, armed with bows and arrows, lances, tomahawks and knives, on either side of the stream, and confidently awaited the invaders.

" As soon as it was dusk five large canoes loaded with 100 selected warriors started down the stream, and as there was a strong current it was not long before they fell into the trap. The leading canoes were successively swamped before their occupants could realize the nature of the obstruction. The cries of their unfortunate companions, however, enabled those in the last two canoes to

reach the shore before coming to the log. In the meantime thirty of the occupants of the leading canoes were either drowned, killed or captured by Sealth's
warriors, and those who reached shore in safety betook themselves up the river
again, and their account of the disaster which had befallen their companions
so discouraged the remainder of the expedition that they retired to their mountain homes.

" When Sealth and his warriors returned to the bay with such substantial
proofs of the victory gained over their former persecutors great was the rejoic-
ing among the salt water tribes and the hero of the hour was the young warrior who, by his cleverness, boldness and courage, had delivered them from a
great danger. A grand council of the tribes was called, composed of the chiefs
and leading warriors and medicine men from the following six tribes : Old-
Man-House, Moxliepush, Duwamish, Black River, Shilshole and Lake, whose
chiefs were Kitsap, Seattle Curley, Tecumseh, Salmon Bay Curley and Lake
John, Seattle Curley being chief of both the Moxliepush and the Duwamish
tribes. At this council Sealth was made great chief of all the tribes and the
former chiefs became tyees, or sub-chiefs. The Moxliepush, Black River and
Lake tribes, however, did not consent to a consolidation and Sealth, having
assumed the authority conferred upon him by the majority, determined to
make his authority respected by all. He organized an expedition composed of
the bravest of his followers and made a tour of the three rebellious tribes,
going by way of Shilshole and Salmon bays, Lake Union and across the port-
age to Lake Washington and thence to Black river and back to Old-Man-
House. Though prepared to give battle if necessary he subdued his opponents by diplomacy. He held councils at various places on his route, made
speeches to the tribesmen and won them over from their chiefs, and when they
had submitted he took a number of hostages from each tribe along with him.
In this way he gained the submission of all the rebellious chiefs and tribesmen
without fighting a battle or killing a man. When the first white man came
here Chief Sealth had quite a number of these hostages, who were called slaves
by the other Indians, but who were not treated any differently, so far as the
whites could observe, than the other Indians. Indeed, many of these so-called
slaves afterwards became Chief Sealth's principal lieutenants.

" After Chief Sealth had consolidated the tribes and enforced his right to the
chieftainship, he still further strengthened his influence over the tribes by
checking other raids by unfriendly tribes from the north and south, and concluded treaties of friendship with them. He even carried his wise rule so far
as to anticipate the formation of the Chinook language by the Hudsons Bay
traders by so adapting the several distinct dialects then prevailing amongst the
different tribes scattered over a large area, that at length they could converse
with one another, where before they could not. Thus he brought about the

formation of a language common to all the tribes from the Snohomish and Sno-qualmie as far south and west as Olympia.

" By his great exploits in war, his wisdom and prudence in council, and the nobility of his character, Chief Sealth obtained a wonderful influence over all the natives in this section, whether belonging to his tribes or to others. And thus it was that, when I first saw him, his deep voice, slow and grave speech were listened to with such marked deference and respect by all. He was the supreme arbiter in their disputes, and his decisions were accepted as final and conclusive and carried out with unquestioning obedience. Having early been converted to the Catholic faith, he introduced and successfully carried out many moral reforms among his people. He reprimanded them often for drunkenness, fighting and their loose sexual relations with the whites. He was a great peacemaker and always avoided bloodshed whenever possible. He even undertook to subvert the ancient traditional customs of his race in regard to bloody retaliation for mortal wrongs, and to inculcate among his people Christian principles.

" Though a man of great natural abilities, Chief Sealth never learned either the Chinook or the English languages ; nor did any of the older Indians whom I knew. An interpreter was always necessary whenever any of the whites wished to converse with him. In appearance he was dignified, but somewhat bent with age when I knew him, and at that time he always walked with a staff in his hand. He looked like a superior man among his people. Though the top of his head had been flattened in childhood, the malformation was not so apparent as it was in all the other old Indians of his day. During the summer months and when I first saw him he wore but a single garment. That was a Hudsons Bay company's blanket, the folds of which he held together with one hand, and from their midst appeared the broad chest and strong arm of bronze which grasped his staff. The sketch herewith represented the old chief as he appeared on the streets of Seattle thirty-four years ago.

" The later years of Chief Sealth were passed at his headquarters at the Old-Man-House in Kitsap county, near Port Madison, and in visiting the tribes, administering justice, reproof and counsel to his devoted people. He was often in Seattle, where he was respected by all the white people. The Old-Man-House, where he resided was a famous gathering place for the natives from all over the Sound, and some of the potlatches held there have been attended by as many as 8,000 Indians. I saw one there at which there was fully 1,500 present.

" After a long illness, during which the old chief was frequently visited by natives and early white settlers from all over the Sound, he died at the Old-Man-House. His funeral was attended by several hundred white people and by more of his own people. G. A. Meigs, proprietor of the Port Madison mill, shut down his mill and on his steamer took all the employes and others over to the funeral. A great many also went over from Seattle. As the old chief was a Catholic he was buried with the ceremonies of that church, mingled with which were customs peculiar to the natives. The ceremonies were imposing and impressive, and the chanting of the litanies by the native singers was very beautiful.

" During his life Chief Sealth had two or three successive wives, but he did not have many children.

" Princess Angeline was his only child by his first wife. When I first knew her she was a washerwoman for the white people, among whom she was a great favorite, and although she was a buxom widow and not bad-looking, she was always esteemed as a virtuous, good woman, She had a daughter who married a half-breed, and by whom she had a son, now living, named Joe Foster. His parents died early and old Angeline has reared him, slaved for him and begged for him. She has gotten him out of many scrapes and her whole heart is wrapped up in the boy, 'My papa's great-grandchild.'

" Angeline had a half-sister who married a chief on Lake Samamish and died some time ago, but I don't know any more about her. I think Chief Sealth also left by his last wife a son, who is now living at Old-Man-House. This son has a grandson there who is a dwarf. He is 20 years old and is only thirty inches tall, is very bright, well formed, talks English and is the pet of all the Indians on the reservation.

" During the past thirty-three years I have on many occasions endeavored to learn from the oldest and most intelligent Indians something of their earlier recollections ; for instance as to when the heaviest earthquake occurred. They said that one is said to have occurred a great many years before any white men had ever been seen here, when mam-ook ta-mahn-a-wis was carried on by hundreds. This is the same performance they go through when they are making medicine men, and consists of shouting, singing, beating on the drums and sticks and apparently trying to make as much noise as they can. While making a medicine man I have seen upwards of 100 painted Indians driving on the streets here a young man stripped nearly naked, with a long lariat fastened to a girdle around his waist. At one time it took them over a week to make a ta-mahn-a-wis man of the fellow they were driving. After he became supernaturally fixed he came near dying, and old Dr. Maynard, the only physician then in town, was called in to give him a dose of civilized medicine.

" The only total eclipse of the sun visible here during the past thirty-four years occurred about twenty-five years ago during a clear afternoon. The white settlers were preparing their smoked glasses. Ex-Chief Lake John happened to come by about that time, and I told him in Chinook that the sun was to be darkened in about an hour from that time. He very sharply inquired how I knew, and I told him I was in klosh tum-tum with the Sah-ha-le tyee, or that I was on good terms with God. He laughed heartily at such a ridiculous notion, but when the sun began to be obscured I handed him a piece of smoked glass, and after looking through it he became very grave, and looking at the sky in amazement he said with great seriousness, ' De-late mi-ka cum-tux,' you have told the truth. When the eclipse became total the howling and pounding of drums over at Plummer's point, where the Indians were assembled, could be heard all over town.

" In 1880, when the deep snow occurred in January, there being over four feet of the beautiful, I inquired of an old Indian if he had ever seen snow so deep before, and he said no, but that his father had told him that there was one fall of snow many years before which was equal to it. Lake Union has been frozen all over twice, and a number of times has formed two to five inches thick in sheltered places of the lake. Only twice since 1856 has it been as cold as it was this winter.

" A son of Pat Kanim, the old chief of the Snoqualmies, who now lives on the Tulalip reservation, told me that his father had been a good, true friend of the whites during the Indian war, and he corroborated what A. A. Denny has said in his history of that war. He said that Mr. Denny had with good reason placed confidence in his father, notwithstanding that others thought he was not worthy of it. He said that Leschi and Nelson were the leaders in the massacre near Slaughter, where eight whites were killed in 1855. These were the same tribes that had attempted the raid fifty years before which Chief Sealth foiled, and the same which attacked the town of Seattle in 1856. This time they came across Lake Washington instead of down the river, landing their canoes where is now located Leschi park. They had not forgotten Seatth's plan of resisting an invasion by the river route."

To Dr. Maynard it is said belongs the honor of naming the city of Seattle after the old chief and also of conferring the name Angeline on his daughter.

There is one descendant of the old chief who is at once the pride and the one particular character of the Queen City today. That descendant is Angeline, daughter of the old chief; Princess Angeline she is called. She is not courtly or noble in bearing and never showed any superior powers of intellect, indeed, it is not saying too much to say that to the present residents who know her she does not exhibit even average Indian intelligence, though great and enfeebled old age may in a measure account for it. Angeline had a revelation last year when she was shown a painting of the old chief, life size and true to the original. It is said of her that at least she showed that she had a tender memory and soft heart, for she cried and went about the streets muttering in her Indian way : " Utch-i-dah, utch-i-dah ; nika papa hias klosh." Wonderful ! wonderful ! good picture of Sealth.

Poor old Angeline. Bent, decrepit and carrying the weight of 80 years with an effort, she still possessed a heart full of tenderness that could only find relief in a flood of tears.

Long, long ago it had been that old Angeline saw the royal old chieftain, her father, for the last time. Only in her Indian memory had she communed with him who was once lord of all around in the neighborhood of Elliott bay. But now she stood face to face once more and looked into the kindly face of the old chief, who has been dead these many years. It was Chief Sealth, life size, as he appeared thirty-five or forty years ago, with his big, blue-bordered Hudsons Bay company blanket hanging in Grecian folds from his dusky shoulders. No wonder poor old Angeline cried and sobbed and broke down in the rush of tender recollections that must have filled her old soul. No wonder she exclaimed : "Utch-i-dah ! utch-i-dah ! nika papa hias klosh."

It was her old-time friend Samuel Coombs, the pioneer, who took old Angeline to see the picture of the old chief, painted by Mr. Coombs' son Raphael for the chamber of commerce of this city. Angeline, the last survivor of the old chief's family, did not know what was wanted of her, but she knew that her old friend meant her no harm and she trudged along, muttering in her peculiar guttural Indian dialect until she came plunk upon the big painting. It shows the old chief as he first appeared to the whites about 40 years ago, standing erect with a big shock of raven hair, a broad face, kindly eye and the picture of a perfect Indian, showing in a marked degree the great intelligence the old chief is known to have possessed. He is as nature found him, bereft of ornament save the big gray blanket with its broad border of blue about his shoulders.

Angeline's judgment ought to be taken as to the merits of the picture. She pronounces it good, very good, and it will probably become the one great memento of the now vanished royal rule that prevailed over the woods and bays and tribes hereabouts before the white man came and took possession. In the perspective of the picture are the snowy lines of the grand Olympic mountains, looking very pretty and true to reality. Angeline leaned against the counter and cried till her Indian tears fell thick and fast. " Nika papa hias klosh," she muttered as she turned away towards the door and then trudged off down the street, but not for long. She trudged back for another look and many times during the afternoon she passed and repassed the window, muttering that it was good, and peeking through the big plate windows, for the picture had been set therein for the passerby to look at. Young Coombs' picture is from a photograph of the old chief furnished by the old pioneer, Hon. A. A. Denny, taken years ago.

To the older settlers Angeline's name was given by some of the Indians as Wee-wy-eke and by herself as Kakii-Silma ; very pretty names both of them.

A daughter of Angeline, known to the whites by the unpretentious name of Betsey, had the prettily sounding Indian name of Che-wa-tum.

There is another little painting by young Coombs, just as full of interest as that of the old chief. It is a reproduction in oil of the old log cabin, the first log cabin built by the white settlers forty or more years ago, on Alki point. The picture is from a sketch taken a dozen years ago while yet the old log hut was in a state of preservation and it is said to be a very realistic likeness. The picture is now the property of Mr. Denny and he treasures it as one of his most valued mementoes.

In his little book, " Pioneer Days on Puget Sound," Mr. Denny, speaking of the first log house says :

" Our first work was to provide shelter for the winter, and we finished the house begun by brother and Lee Terry for J. N. Low, and took shelter in it from the rain, which was falling more or less every day ; but we did not regard it with much concern and seldom lost any time on that account. We next built a log house for myself, which increased our room very materially and made all more comfortable. We had now used up all the timber suitable for log houses, which we could get without a team, and we split cedar and built houses for Bell and Boren, which we considered quite a fancy, but not so substantial as log houses. About the time we had completed our winter quarters, the brig Leonesa, Captain Daniel S. Howard, came to anchor in the bay. Seeing that the place was inhabited by whites, the captain came ashore seeking a cargo of piles, and we readily made a contract to load the vessel. We had no team at the time, but some of us went to work cutting the timber nearest the water, and rolled and hauled in by hand, while Lee Terry went up Sound and obtained a yoke of oxen, which he drove on the beach from Puyallup with which to complete the cargo, but we had made very considerable progress by hand before his arrival.

" Alki point had not been a general camping place for the Indians, but soon after we landed and commenced clearing the land, they commenced to congregate and continued coming until we had over 1,000 in our midst and most of them remained all winter. Some of them built their houses very near ours, even on the ground we had cleared, and although they seemed very friendly towards us, we did not feel safe in objecting to their building, and it was very noticeable that they regarded their proximity to us as a protection against other Indians."

Little more than one generation ago, at a date which would extend quite beyond the date birth of very many people in Seattle, there was assembled on the neck of land known as Elliott point, Alki point, Duwamish head and West Seattle, or as the Indians called it Squ-ducks, a large band of Indians and a great pow wow was going on.

One thousand natives of the Duwamish and other tribes with a few strag-
glers from distant local tribes were assembled and sat about their smouldering
fires, lounged lazily in brown-colored canoes or were snoring under rakish tents
much as the Indians of today do about Ballast island or the hop fields.

All was excitement.

History records the fact that the day was a beautiful one, a brilliant sun
shedding a brilliant light over a most primeval and rural scene.

Over all this vast congregation of God's simple-minded children there ruled

OLDEST HOUSE IN KING COUNTY—J. W. MAPLE'S, WHITE RIVER

a chief—old Chief Sealth—then a patriarch, aged, yet stately and dignified;
an Indian simple and untutored, though yet an orator of the highest rank.

Old Chief Sealth, a name honored and revered even at that early day; a
name since become historic and wreathed with an enduring, undying fame.

It was at a day when the flames of Indian warfare were beginning to smoul-
der after a long seige of war, of ambush and bloodshed on Puget Sound, though
the old patriarch of the forest, Chief Sealth, had refrained from lending a hand
in the bloody work of his tribal relations and neighbors. He, like many of

the proud chieftains in the earlier settlement of the Atlantic and middle states, stood by the white men—the invaders we might say—when their brethren wore the war paint and carried the scalp-lock at their girdle.

On this historic day old Sealth sat gloomily down in front of his wigwam waiting in stolid indifference for the coming of the Boston man, who was to treat with him that day and bring him news from the great white chief at Washington.

At last the great white chief's agent, Colonel M. T. Simmons, made his appearance, coming from the direction of Olympia, and landed in front of the staid old Siwash chief's camp. The ceremony of an introduction was gone through with in the Chinook jargon, Colonel Simmons being a master in that tongue, and being an emissary of the government of much repute among the Indians.

We can imagine the old chief receiving in his dignified, though simple style, this messenger from the government. We of today might clothe our imagination with the vision of Princess Angeline, the old chief's daughter, then a maiden of comely, though dusky, looks, standing respectfully near and listening, possibly in eagerness, to this bartering away of her father's domain—her own heritage—to the stranger.

Princess Angeline now broken and enfeebled by 40 years of care and bitter memories, yet lives by that same seaside and almost within sight of the identical spot whereon that great pow wow was held. Well for poor old Angeline that her sensibilities are stunted and seared, that time has graciously smothered any remembrance of those days of freedom, when none but her people and kindred owned and traversed these woods and waters.

But to the story.

Colonel Simmons had left Olympia on the 15th day of May, 1858, to visit the several Indian tribes on Puget Sound and conclude the treaties with them and arrange for the disbursement of annuities and provisions. The commissioner had first called at Fort Kitsap, G. A. Page local agent, where some 400 Indians waited for him. Colonel Simmons, after the preliminaries necessary for such an august occasion, was the first to address the assemblage of chiefs and Indians. His speech was in Chinook and no interpreter was needed. He referred to the promises that had been made and which were about to be realized, and wound up with the reference at the close of his speech to the propensities of the Indian for rum and the evil effects therefrom.

The venerable old chief being first in authority among the assembled red men, was the first to speak. With the dignity becoming the occasion and the position of a great chief, he arose, wrapped his heavy blanket more closely about his shoulders, and began his address. The reference of Colonel Simmons to the Indian thirst for strong drink touched the old man's quick, though he did not show it by any outward sign or expression of feature. No, old Chief Sealth was too august, too grand for that. Colonel Simmons would learn of his displeasure, but in a manner and with weapons of his own choice. Sealth would show that he was an orator. Translated, he said :

"I am not a bad man ; I want you to understand what I say ; I do not drink rum ; neither does New-E-Chis, (another chief present) and we continually advise our people not to do so.

"I am and always have been a friend to the whites. I listen to what Mr. Page (the resident agent) says to me, and I do not steal nor do any of my people steal from the whites.

"Oh, Mr. Simmons, why do not our papers come back to us ? You always say they will come back, but they do not come. I fear that we are forgotten or that we are to be cheated out of our land.

"I have been very poor and hungry all winter and am very sick now. In a little while I will die. I should like to be paid for my lands before I die. Many of my people died during the cold winter without getting their pay. When I die my people will be very poor—they will have no property, no chief and no one to talk for them. You must not forget them, Mr. Simmons, when I am gone.

"We are ashamed when we think of the Puyallups, as they have now got their papers. They fought against the whites whilst we, who have never been angry with them, get nothing. When we get our pay we want it in money. The Indians are not bad. It is the mean white men that are bad to them. If any person writes that we do not want our papers they tell lies.

"Oh, Mr. Simmons ; you see I am sick, I want you to write quickly to the great chief what I say. I am done."

Then the old chief retired. Calm his mein, unruffled his spirits, dignified his tirade, though age had bent his stately bearing, for old Chief Sealth had even then—long before that day when he arose to call in question the integrity of a great nation which had promised to pay him for his birthright and had not done so—passed the milestones on life's great highway, when man's and Indian's, too, allotted days of labor are over.

It was the same old story. The dominion of the untutored child of the forest had been usurped by the ruthless hand of civilization and the Indian life had been crushed out.

It had followed the red man from the bleak New England shore to a last great stand on the borders of the western sea. Chief Sealth, like Powantonimo, Red Jacket, Black Hawk, Tecumseh and all the great line of chiefs of the American red man, had given up their ancestral possessions to the pale faces and was ready to die of a broken heart.

On the evening of the same day (May 15) Simmons and party reached

DUKE OF YORK

Skagit Head, under Captain R. C. Fay, where some 800 Indians of the tribes of Skagits, Snohomish, Snoqualmies and others were assembled. He made about the same speech to them as at Fort Kitsap, when Hetty Kannim, a sub-chief, answered him as follows :

" I am but a sub-chief, but I am chosen for my people to speak for them today. I will speak what I think and I want any of the drinking Indians to contradict me if they can. Liquor is killing our people off fast. Our young men spend their money and their work for it. Then they get angry and kill each other and sometimes kill their wives and children. We old men do not drink and we beg our boys to not trade with cultus (bad) Boston men for liquor. We have all agreed to tell our agent when any liquor boats are about

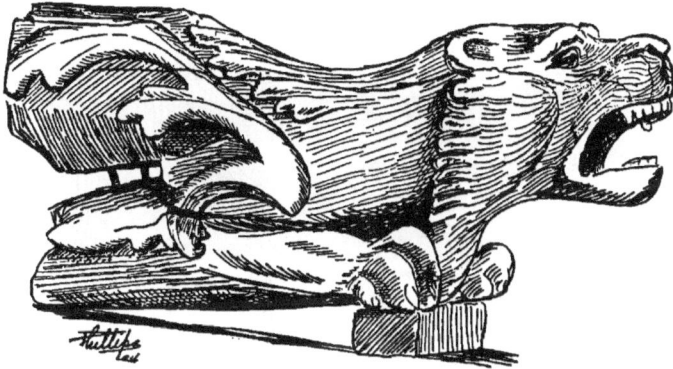

EAST INDIAN CARVING, FIGUREHEAD BARK ENTERPRISE

and help to arrest the man who sells it. I will now talk about our treaties. When is the Great Father who lives across the mountains going to send us our papers back ? Four summers have passed since you and Governor Stevens told us we would get our pay for lands. We remember well what you said to us over there (pointing to Elliott bay) and our hearts are very sick because you did not do as you promised. We saw the Puyallups and the Nisquallys get their annual pay and our hearts were sick because we could get nothing. We never fought with the whites. We considered it good to have good white people among us. Our young women can gather berries and clams and our young men can fish and hunt and sell what they get to the whites. We are willing that the whites shall take the timber, but we want the game and the fish and we want our homes, where there is plenty of game and fish and good lands for potatoes. We want our Great Father to know what our hearts are and we want you to send our talk to him at once. I have done."

"Hiram," a Snoqualmie then spoke :

"We want our treaty to be concluded as soon as possible. We are tired of waiting. Our reason is that our old people, and there are many of them, are dying. Look at those old men and women ; they have only a little while to live and they want to get their pay for their lands. The white people have taken it and you, Mr. Simmons, promised us we should be paid, you and Governor Stevens. Suspense is killing us.

"We are afraid to plant potatoes on the river bottom, lest some bad white man shall come and make us leave. You know what we are Mr. Simmons. You was the first American we ever knew and our children will remember you as long as they remember anything. I was but a boy when I first knew you.

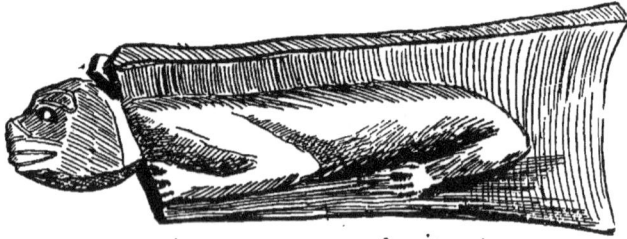

CANOE HEAD TOTEM, SKOKOMISH

You know we do not want to drink liquor, but we cannot help it when the bad Boston man brings it to us and urges us to drink. When our treaties were made we told our hearts to you and Governor Stevens and they have not changed since. I have done."

"Bonaparte," a Snohomish chief, then spoke as follows :

"What I have to say is not of much consequence. My children have all been killed by rum, and I am very poor. I believe what Mr. Simmons tells about our treaty, but most Indians think he lies. My heart is not asleep. I have known Mr. Simmons a long time and he never lied to me, and I think he will tell the Great Father that we want to get our pay. I have done."

The Indians at Point no Point were then seen and many speeches of a like character were made and then the party returned to Olympia.

CHAPTER XXX

THE MAKAH TRIBE

In the extreme northwestern portion of the United States outside of Alaska, around and about the base of that sightly headland Cape Flattery, where it has been said in a spirit of half jest, but worth taking most seriously, that never a day in the year passes without rain, dwells a small nation of men and women who will go down in history, in song and story perhaps, as a happy, contented people ; a people doubly fortunate in the possession of a unique territory abounding with fruits of land and sea. Back of them are the mountains, their front door yard the rollicking, boundless expanse of frothy ocean; fish in the one, fowl and meat in the other. Under their feet are the white sands of the ocean beach, and over them seems continually to watch a most magnanimous providence. These people are the Makah Indians, robust, ruddy, big brothers and big sisters, whose other branch of the family undoubtedly exists on the further side of the Straits of Juan de Fuca, so much do the general characteristics of the one with the other seem to run together.

The Makah Indians are many generations advanced in civilization to that of some of the Sound tribes. Why this is so is — because it is so. They have enjoyed no greater privileges than other tribes. They are in fact further removed than most tribes from civilizing influences that have prevailed in the last generation. Perchance in this very fact lies their present condition. Association with whites generally brings the worst of moral results for the Indians whenever the Indian is permitted to be his own or his brother's keeper to any great extent. He readily succumbs to the vices of the white man, but removed from these associations for the greater part of his time and under the guidance of a conscientious agent, the Indian should advance morally and mentally. The infusion of a great deal of white blood into the tribe of the Makah (for some of the earliest settlers went to the Straits to settle) has had a good effect. At present the leading men are largely half-breeds who have been to school and look very intelligent fellows. They are lively and smart in business. They know how to hunt and they know how to fish as no other Washington tribe does. In fact, since the issuance of the decree of pelagic sealing the Indian seal hunters of Neah Bay carry the palm of greatest success in that line. They own schooners but they are not sailors. Somehow the proprietorship of several well known sealing vessels has come to them without any effort on their part; it was something of a parental care on the part of a thoughtful government, and although the average Indian found on board does not know a rat line from a marlin spike they go to sea nevertheless, are blown out and blown in and always bring home seals. When off on long voyages they are usually accompanied by white men with more or less knowledge of sealing and navigation and are not so much at the mercy of their own ignorance of those things. When it comes down to hunting seal or fishing off the coast within sight of land, the Makah asks nothing better than his stout, roomy cedar canoe. He will chase a whale too, as quickly as he will a seal. They are great sea rovers, are the buccaneers of the northwest, and will start off on a three hundred mile voyage in light canoes, down the coast or up the Straits and Sound, with no more serious consideration than if they were going only as far as the nearest bight or inlet. They are a whole community of fishermen, industrious but not frugal. Without money they are contented, with money the reverse. An Indian knows nothing of the value of money beyond the spending of it. The first thing the Indians do after a successful sealing voyage or a trip to the hop fields where men, women and children unite in gathering the hops, is to repair to the cities and larger towns on the Sound and expend the proceeds in a thousand and one gaudy and useless articles that please the passing fancy of the native. They have however been taught to provide themselves with provisions and manufactured goods for household use, and there are some very comfortable homes upon the reservation.

Judge James G. Swan, of Port Townsend, who is a recognized authority on the Cape Indians recently wrote a very interesting chapter on the Makah Indians which appeared in the *Post-Intelligencer*, of Seattle, and is partially as follows:

"From Neah Bay to the Pacific coast in a southwest direction is a prairie through which runs a creek which empties into the Pacific ocean at the Indian village Wa-atch, four miles distant from Neah Bay. A few miles south of Wa-atch is another village called Tsoo-ess, and south of this is another village called Ho-sett or Osette. These three villages with the village at Neah Bay constitute the winter residences of the Makah tribe of Indians. During the summer months they move to villages nearer Cape Flattery, one of which is at Kiddecubbut, a few miles west of Neah Bay, another is on Tatoosh island, and a third at Archawat, on the coast near Wa-atch, so as to be near the halibut banks, the whaling grounds and the fine seal fishing. In 1859, when I first visited Neah Bay, the Makah tribe numbered 820 persons, 220 of whom were strong men or 'braves,' and the remainder women, children and slaves. Their means of subsistence were almost entirely drawn from the ocean, and at that time their principal food was dried halibut, dried whale blubber and oil, salmon, true cod, Gadus morhua, cultus cod, Ophiodon elongatus, black cod or beshow, Anoplopoma fimbria, with various other kinds of smaller fish, and shell fish of different kinds, such as mussels, crabs, clams, cockles, limpets, sea slugs and snales, octopus, squid and barnacles. Of late years they have accustomed themselves to some of the white man's food, such as flour, hard bread, rice, beans and potatoes, and, like other Indians, are very fond of molasses or syrup, which they eat with their bread and rice; but all their other food is usually greased with a plentiful supply of whale oil. I have frequently eaten with them, and must confess that dried halibut dipped in fresh sweet whale oil is not an objectionable repast to a hungry man.

"The whale blubber is cut in strips, then boiled to extract the oil which is carefully skimmed off, and after being boiled again to expel the moisture, is put into receptacles for use as food. The blubber after being boiled is hung up in the smoke and dried and looks like bacon.

" The halibut is cut into thin flakes, which are dried in the sun without salt, and when well cured is nice, either eaten dry, dipped in whale oil or simply boiled or toasted before the fire.

" The Makahs are particularly dextrous in handling their canoes, and proceed in them fearlessly many miles from land in pursuit of whales or seals, or for fishing on the halibut banks fifteen miles northwest from the Cape. Their canoes are beautifully modeled, resembling our finest clipper ships. They are formed from a single log of cedar, carved out with skill and elegance. The best canoes are made by the Clayoquot and Nittinat tribes on Vancouver island, B. C., who sell them to the Makahs, but few being made by the latter tribe, owing to the scarcity of cedar in their vicinity.

" In attacking a whale their canoes are invariably manned with eight men— six to paddle, one to steer and one in the bow to throw the harpoon. The harpoons are either made of hoop iron, old sheathing metal or a flat mussel shell sharpened to a point, having barbs of elk horn fastened on each side of the flat surface of the point, securely bound with wild cherry bark and neatly fastened to a stout lanyard varying in length from one to four fathoms. The whole of the spearhead is smeared over with pitch made of spruce gum, to give it smoothness and uniformity of surface. The pole or staff is from fifteen to twenty feet long, tapering at each end, and made of yew, which gives it strength and solidity. When used the lanyard is made fast to a buoy of sealskin taken off whole from the animal and dried with the hair side inward. This is first blown up like a bladder, then the end of the pole is inserted between the barbs and darted into the whale, leaving the pole which is taken back into the canoe. The short lanyard is used when striking the whale in the head, and has only one buoy attached.   The long one is used in striking the body and has three buoys to it. When a number of these buoys are fastened to a whale, he is obliged to remain at or near the surface of the water and is easily killed with spears and long lances.   Seals and porpoises are killed with similarly formed harpoons, but much smaller.

"'Their fishing lines are made of the stem of the gigantic kelp, Nereocystis, which is common along the northwest coast.   This kelp, commencing at its root in a slender stem about the size of a pipe stem, or codline, rises to within a few fathoms of the surface of the water with but little increase of size, and then gradually enlarges till it terminates in a hollow knob or bulb, which always floats on the surface of the water, and from this bulb issue long streamer-like leaves fifteen or twenty feet long.   The Indians cut off the long slender portion of the stem, then soak it in fresh running water three or four days, or until it turns white, and then stretch it and rub it to a uniform size, then knot the pieces together, coil them up and the fish line is made.   When dry it is brittle and readily broken, but an immersion in water a few minutes makes it pliable, when it becomes tough and exceedingly strong.   The bulb of this kelp and upper part of the stem being hollow, are used for various purposes.   Fish-bait is kept in them, and the larger ones are frequently used as water bottles.

" The fishhooks of the Makahs are made of the knots or butt parts of hem-lock limbs first split into splinters of the required length and whittled to the re-quired shape, then placed in a kelp stem and roasted in hot ashes till pliable, then bent into a form like an ox bow.   The line is fastened to the upper arm, and on the inside of the lower arm a barb of bone is firmly attached, and with this rude and simple instrument they readily secure the halibut and cod.   For smaller fish they use steel fishhooks purchased of the white men.

" The houses or lodges of the Makahs are built of cedar boards and planks and are usually of large size, eighteen to twenty feet high and forty to sixty feet square, with slightly elevated shed-like roofs.   These boards are split from cedar logs with little wedges of yew and require skill and patience to make them.   These houses are comfortable dwellings, excepting the smoke, and as they have several families in each lodge, each family having a separate fire the smoke of which serves to dry the fish and blubber, the usual fumes cause an in-tense smarting in the eyes of visitors who are not accustomed to so much carbon in the atmosphere.   During the past ten years some of the better class of Indi-ans at Neah village have built houses in white men's style, but all the older villages retain the ancient form of building.

" Their manufactures consist of such implements as are used in fishing and hunting — harpoons, spears, bows and arrows and fishhooks.   Bows and arrows are now rarely used except by the boys for shooting birds, the Hudsons Bay company musket taking its place, and of late years rifles and double-barreled shotguns; the women braid mats very neatly from cedar bark and weave blankets from dogs' hair. Baskets and conical-shaped Chinese-looking hats for keeping off rain, are made from spruce roots, cedar twigs and bleached bear grass. They also make of these materials, table mats which are very handsome and durable. The northern Indians and particularly those of Queen Charlotte island, B. C., are very expert carvers of wood and stone, and manufacture bracelets, finger rings and ear ornaments of silver and gold, decorated with carvings of various devices. The tribe south of Queen Charlotte group have little skill in these particulars, and only carve rude faces of men or animals of their mythology on their masks and other articles.

"The Makahs are fond of music, and many of their songs and chants, when sung in chorus, are melodious and musical. They readily pick up tunes from others and can sing the popular songs of the day, and some of the scholars at the agency school learned to play the piano and organ; in fact they can learn anything that white children are taught.

"The primitive dress of the Makahs at the time of establishing the reservation in 1862 was simple and picturesque. During warm weather a blanket was the usual covering of both sexes, the women simply adding a cotton skirt or petticoat, or a cincture of cedar bark spun into a coarse fringe, reaching from the waist to the knee. Some of the men tied their hair into a club knot behind, around which they wore a wreath of hemlock or spruce twigs or fresh plucked sea weed, giving them a picturesque appearance. During rains or cold weather the men wore bearskin cloaks, with the head part cut off so that the forepaws can be brought on each side of the neck and fastened; the paws, with the great nails attached, hang down upon the breast. On their heads they place the conical-shaped hat painted with various designs, and in this costume, with the addition of a gun or spear, they make a formidable appearance. Both sexes have the cartilage of the nose pierced, and into this is tied a pendant piece of abalone shell by way of ornament. Shell ear ornaments were also worn, but now are but seldom seen. The females ornament themselves when in full dress for dancing or ceremonial purposes, with a coronet made of the dentalium, or tooth shell, called 'haiqua.' This is fastened around the head in parallel rows, and its pearly whiteness contrasted with their black hair is very ornamental. Into their ears are fastened strings of haiqua, intermingled with brass buttons, thimbles, beads of various colors and pieces of the green shells of the abalone. Rings of brass wire encircle the wrists, bunches of beads of various colors are tied around the neck, and strings of beads wound around the ankles; the line of the parting of the hair on the top of the head is marked with vermillion, the eyebrows blackened with charcoal, the face is greased with deer's fat and then rubbed over with vermillion, and this was the ornamental appearance of a Makah belle when on dress parade.

'' When about their usual work among fish and blubber, or when they are off on a trading voyage with a load of oil and dried halibut, their.dress is very simple and very dirty. I have seen many of the men with a coating of grease and soot covering their entire bodies, and the dresses of the women completely saturated with oil and dirt; but as soon as they get through their work or return from a cruise up Fuca straits there is a general washing. This washing scene is the usual morning ceremony. They are very fond of bathing in the surf, and do not omit their bath even in the coldest weather.

'' Breakfast immediately follows the bath, and as all their meals are served alike, a description of one at which I partook in 1859 will give an idea of the style then prevalent. On entering the lodge I was invited to sit down near the chief or head man of the family. His portion of the lodge was separated from the rest of the building by a screen of mats to keep off the cold: Before me, circled round the fire, were the children and slaves, for slavery existed among them at that time, and on the raised platform sat the principal members of the family. At my left, suspended from a pole stuck in the ground, hung the cradle of an infant who was firmly lashed in an oblong basket, and its head compressed by bark and moss bound tightly across its forehead. The mother, sitting near, lulled the child to sleep by gently pulling a string tied to the top of the pole, producing a motion not unlike a modern baby jumper. Around the sides of the lodge were boxes and chests of the occupants, and on shelves over these were piled baskets of potatoes and dried fish and skins of oil; overhead hung blubber and fish to dry in the smoke for future food. The meal consisted of roasted potatoes, boiled ducks, boiled fish, dried halibut and whale oil. Hard bread and molasses were offered me, but I declined, thinking that whale oil was more of a rarity to my palate. The viands were served up in wooden trenchers, and all helped themselves without any aid from knife or fork. When we had finished, we wiped our greasy hands and faces on some cedar bark, beat into a soft, fibrous mass, called ' tupsoc,' and rinsed our mouths with a drink of cold water. They usually take three meals a day, excepting when they have a feasting time when they go from house to house eating at every one. On one occasion when I was taking the census of the tribe, I was invited to partake of food in each lodge I visited. As that was impossible I asked my interpreter what I should do, as to refuse hospitality is to give offense. ' Oh,' said he, ' all you have to do is to put your finger down your throat as we do, and thus relieve you stomach.' And that really is the only alternative, and with Indians it is very effective, as I have seen an Indian apparently eat with relish seven or eight breakfasts, but somehow I never could acquire the practice, and I was excused, as I was a white man.

'' Among the old Indians and those who have not been educated, these old customs prevail, but with the younger generation who have attended school, the habits of civilization are followed in a degree. The Makah Indian agency was established in June, 1862, with Henry A. Webster United States Indian agent. I was appointed teacher and superintendent of the government building, and remained until August, 1866. My first pupil was a bright little boy about nine years old named James Claplanhoo, the hereditary chief of the tribe. Jimmie remained with me all the time I was on the reservation, and then went to live with the Indian agent as cook until he was old enough to marry, and then he married one of the schoolgirls, Mary Ann Charliquoa, and has a family of boys and girls. His eldest son, Jorji James, is captain of the sealing schooner Deeahks, and his eldest daughter, Minnie, is married to Chistoqua Peterson, one of the smartest young men in the tribe, a graduate of the Indian school, who owns the sealing schooner Columbia and is a regular trader.

"The Makahs are a self-supporting and thrifty tribe. When I went among them to reside officially, the largest vessels they had were canoes dug out of cedar logs, and they were the most expert surfmen I have seen. I advised them to get larger vessels and the government encouraged them, and in 1888 the United States marshal sold to Chistoqua Peterson, Peter Brown and John Tainsub, all Makahs, the seized schooner Anna Beck, of sixty tons gross measurement, which they named the James G. Swan. In 1880 Peter bought the old schooner Letitia and sold her to some Vancouver island Indians and bought the fine schooner Champion, which was lost on Vancouver island. James Claplanhoo bought the pilot boat Lottie, but she was wrecked. He now owns the schooners Deeahks and Emmet Felitz. Lighthouse Jim owns the C. C. Perkins. Yokum, the storekeeper owns the Matilda. The Puritan and August and several smaller sloops and boats are owned by others. During all the 'hard times' this thrifty tribe has made a comfortable living by sealing, whaling and fish-ing for halibut, cod and other varieties. Several of these Indians, such as Capt. James Claplanhoo, Chistoqua Peterson, Peter Brown, Shobid Hunter and others, have comfortable homes like white people, and Kobal runs the only hotel at Neah, which now looks like a little watering village, but the old Indians and those who live in villages on the coast prefer their large wooden lodges, and it will take another generation or more before they will abandon their old customs and adopt the white man's style of living. But they show a degree of industri-ous thrift which could be profitably emulated by croakers and idlers in all our towns."

CHAPTER XXXI

Antedating the first arrivals of white people to the Sound in the 40's, were found in various parts of the country numbers of things showing that white men or civilized or half-civilized people of some color had visited the country. One instance particularly was the remains or indications of a settlement or camp at the mouth of the Duwamish river. As nearly as good judgment could fix it, this camp must have been located at the beginning of the present century. It is not improbable that at some very early day, some navigator bold built a new one or repaired very materially a sailing vessel at that place. Stumps of trees that showed they had been cut for scores of years were found, and the trees themselves gone; strong proof that whoever stopped there did so for a purpose, executed it and went on their way, leaving nothing behind by which their identity could be made known to those who came after them. The Indians had no recollection or tradition of those who cut the trees, though it is not improbable that some one of the early navigators shortly subsequent to Vancouver tarried there for a time.

Another find of later years was the uncovering of a strange and very old cave, an old tomb in one of the public streets of Seattle.

There was not line or marble, nor carving, trinket, old coin nor scroll to tell its history, to name its day. It was way back in the palmy days of 1872 when the old tomb was unearthed and once more saw the light. The toilers of that day were grading down to the virgin soil and carrying Front street to the north. In their path at a spot opposite where the Frye block now stands and just north of Marion street stood a small mound. It must be cut down, and cut down it was; and the dirt carried to a distance south of the present crossing at Marion street and dumped into a small ravine or depression through which an old log-run threaded its course to the higher ground. In the digging of the mound the workmen laid bare the old tomb; and such a tomb! In the center of the mound it was about five feet from the surface. Built up for two or three feet with four walls of stone, boulders from here and there, but in a way showing rudimentary knowledge of architecture and design. Inside was the half-mummy, half-skeleton of some one unknown. Filling all of the space of the sarcophagus was beach sand, apparently having been procured with great care and toil. Such was the story of the unknown dead. It astonished the local historian of that day as it is still the wonder of those same historians who are yet living here today. The old tomb was at least 100 yards from the then high tide line, and the carefully gathered white beach sand had most certainly been carried over the intervening distance from sea to grave. Some joints of the skeleton were decayed, others not. The skull was perfect and what caused the local historian to wonder, and wonder, and wonder again, was that the poll of the skeleton was not flattened. For 20 years after the whites settled here, and. for times out of mind before that the Indians of the Sound had universally flattened the skull. But then it was not Indian, why? Because the Indians said it was not. Old Kitsap's people said it was not, and the traditions and customs of all the local Indians disproved such a proposition. It was on the edges of the high bluffs around the bay, just underneath the grass roots and tufts that clung to the very edges of the bluffs, where the Indian dead were buried, had always been buried, and even up to the present winter days of 1895, when an unusually heavy rainfall may occur, the bones of the dead Indians may be found at odd spots along the bluffs. They never put their dead under ground. The local historian has two probable theories for the cave. In Vancouver's first explorations of the Sound his ships anchored off Blakeley rocks ; after coursing Admiralty inlet Lieu. Puget took a boat's crew and paddled away even to a greater distance up the Sound. Naturally they would explore such a pretty bay as that around the rim of which the Queen City so proudly sits, and it might have been that one of his men died and was buried here. Lewis and Clark's men or some early explorers may have ventured down the valley of the Duwamish river in the dawn of the present century. Trees had been cut and the stumps were still standing that marked the sites of the early camping grounds, and axes had been used in the cutting. It might have been one of those explorers bold, died and was buried in the stone grave so carefully arranged to preserve the bones placed within. But these are only theories and the wonder of the little mound will perhaps forever remain a riddle unsolved.

CHAPTER XXXII

The beauty and grandeur of the great body of water forming the inland sea known to the Pacific coast Indians as the Whulge, attracted many tribes living at some distance from it both in the interior and to the north. Among these visitors were what were always spoken of by the earlier settlers as the Northern Indians. It is now known that these were the tribes from both the British Columbia and Alaska coasts — the Haidas, the most advanced tribe probably in the entire northwest; the T'Klinkets of Alaska, and other less distinguished tribes.

The Haidas occupied principally the Queen Charlotte islands and the Prince of Wales archipelago. There is nothing unusual about these islands in topographical appearance. They present the same broken surface, snow-capped mountains and deep canyons, with huge landslides and sparkling glacial aspect so common in that region. But these same islands of summer rains and fogs and winter ice and snow are peopled by one of the most remarkable races of aborigines found on the American continent. Like nearly all of the rest of the Indians of the northwest coast, they live by hunting and fishing, and as the lands inhabited by them are rough and broken, and subdivided into such small tracts by the numerous mountain ranges, their only means of travel is by water.

The Indians about Dixon entrance are unquestionably superior in physique to the coast Indians to the southward, and among themselves the physical superiority rests with the Haida. This may be due to real ethnical differences, but is probably accounted for in the fact that natural conditions in the Queen Charlotte islands and around such an exposed arm as Dixon entrance have produced a finer and more robust people than those in less exposed regions. While there is considerable uniformity in the general physical character of all the stocks on the northwest coast, a practiced eye can readily detect the difference between them.

As the superiority of the Haidas to the T'Klinkets and Tsimshians comprises the greatest difference in physical characteristics, so with the emotional and moral nature of the three races, the greatest difference is marked only by the superior sensitiveness of the Haidas.

It is in the intellect, however, that the greatest gulf exists between them. One visiting the Haidas sees many strikingly intelligent and attractive faces amongst the older men and women, where experience has given character to their expressions. The dullness attributed to the Indians of the interior here gives place to a more alert expression of countenance. They acquire knowledge readily, and since schools have been established among them their children have made fair progress. They learn all trades with readiness, and before the missionaries and traders came among them they exhibited much ingenuity, not only in the erection of comfortable dwelling houses, but in their numerous carvings on wood and slate, their working and engraving on copper and the erection of those great totem columns which make every Haida village famous.

Their ingenious methods of hunting and fishing, their modes of living, their food, their methods of warfare and their laws and customs are all interesting subjects, but space will make it necessary to confine the present article to some of their totem columns, carvings and engravings.

But little is generally known of the real meaning of these great columns that form such a prominent feature in the Haida settlements. Government experts have been among them during the summer months of several seasons and studied them as thoroughly as possible at such seasons of the year. Judge James G. Swan, of Port Townsend, has also gathered a valuable and complete collection of Haida carvings, engravings, basket work, implements, etc., for the Smithsonian Institution, but thus far there has been but little attention given to the systematic study of the mythology of the race, as that can only be studied with satisfaction during the winter months when the natives are collected in their various homes, thus rendering it possible for only a few of the more inquisitive missionaries and traders to know anything of the legends that compose the rich folklore of the Haida nation. A totem is a rude picture or carving as of a bird or other animal, used as a symbol of a family. It represents a class of material objects which a savage regards with superstitious respect, believing that there exists between him and every member of the class an intimate and altogether special relation. The connection between a man and his totem is beneficial one to the other; the totem protects the man and in return he shows his respect by not killing it, if it be an animal, and by not cutting or gathering it if it be a plant.

There are at least three kinds of totems, namely the clan totem, sex totem and individual totem. The clan totem is common to a whole clan and passes by inheritance from one generation to another, while the individual totem belongs to but one person and does not pass to his descendants.

From their nature totems are constantly undergoing change. Clans tend to become phrateries, split up into sub-phrateries; sub-phrateries decay and finally disappear. An individual becomes wealthy or otherwise distinguishes himself, and being one of the leading men of the tribe, his totem, or rather his crest or sub-totem, which may previously have been an obscure one, rises with him as he advances in importance in his tribe. Under his successors, the totem widens in its numbers and influence, and finally eclipses other clan totems, which in time melt away, or are incorporated with it.

A single system of totems extends throughout the different tribes of the Haidas. The principal totems found among them are the eagle, wolf, crow, black bear, brown bear and thrasher.

The sub-totem usually comes from naming the child after some natural objects from some accidental circumstance or fanciful resemblance, or in nicknaming in after life.

The Haida Indians of Houkan often repeat a legend of a great war between them and the T'Klinkets. While they were engaged in a great battle, which afterwards decided the contest, a flock of ravens flew over and perched on the side of the Haidas. And they being victorious, took "Yalth," or the raven, as the totem of the Haida tribes.

The carved columns of the Haidas may be divided into two classes, the totemic and the commemorative. Those erected in front of houses are usually very tall ones, and are for the most part histories of the families who own them. The top figure is usually the clan totem of the chief occupant. Those below may represent totems of his wife and children, the children always taking unto themselves the mother's totem. Sometimes it illustrates some legend closely connected or referring to the owner's totem. Some of them deal with the history of the tribe, while others are purely legendary, but refer to the totem of the owner. None but the wealthy can afford to erect these carved columns, so that one who is rich enough to own one has a prestige that is so desirable among them. As the head of a household he becomes a petty chief in the village. With the Haida, to accumulate sufficient wealth to own a totem pole and rise to the dignity of a petty chief is the leading passion of his soul.

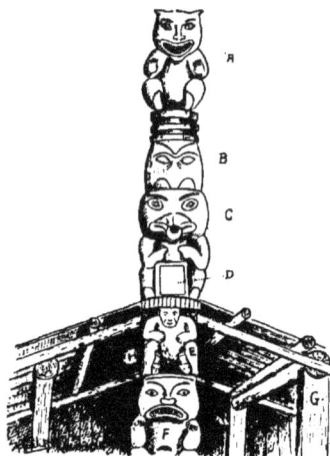

TOTEM COLUMN, NORTHERN INDIANS

Ensign Niblock, of the United States navy, in speaking of these totem columns, says: "A great deal of mystery has been thrown around these pictographic carvings, due to the ignorance and misconception of some writers and the reticence or deliberate deception practiced by the Indians themselves. One of those Indians will not tell his stories or explain his carving to any but the initiated, and then only when they are in perfect sympathy with him. Mr. McLeod, the trader at Houkan, was very successful in gaining information from them that would have been impossible for Mr. Gould, the missionary, or his wife, the government school teacher, to have obtained. Then they have their moods, and will rarely tell their stories either in daytime or during the summer season. But during those long winter nights which characterize that region the old Indian will build a fire and settle himself down in business-like manner and talk as long as the fire lasts. When the fire has burned down to a bed of coals and the dying embers begin to fade away, his story stops. Nor will he build another fire. Nothing more will be heard of the story that night. Thus it often requires a week or more for an old Haida to complete the narration of the story that is written on a single totemic carving.''

Ensign Niblock was quite right when he wrote of these totem carvings: '' They are in no sense idols, but in general may be said to be ancestral columns. The legends which they illustrate are but the traditions, folklore and nursery tales of a primitive people; and while they are in some sense childish or frivolous, and at times even coarse, they represent the current human thought as truly as do the ancient inscriptions in Egypt and Babylonia, or the Maya inscriptions of Yucatan.''

The totemic and commemorative carvings are for the most part symbolical of the objects they represent rather than imitations of them. There is usually some arbitrary mark by which one of the initiated distinguishes one symbol from another. Thus the brown bear is usually known by the peculiar shape of the ears, the beaver by the shape of his teeth, the raven by the sharpness of his bill, the eagle by the shape of his beak, the owl by the ears, the grampus by his great fin, etc.

The explanation of the column in front of the Haida house given in the illustration may be of interest.

The figure (a) at the top of the column represents '' Hoots,'' or the brown bear, which is the totem of the proprietor of the house. The ''disks'' (b) below the bear indicate the high rank or great wealth of the man who erected it. Each one of them usually commemorates some meritorious act of its owner, such as giving a great '' potlatch '' or winning a great victory. Next proceeding down the column is '' Yalth '' (c), the great raven with the moon in his mouth. Beneath him is the bear and hunter (d), and at the bottom is '' Tsing '' (f), the beaver and totem of the wife and children. The following is the story related by the carving of the bear and hunter:

Touats, the hunter, on one occasion visited the house of the great king of

bears. The great bear was not at home, but his wife being there he made love
to her. When Hoots (the bear) returned he found his wife very anxious and
much confused, so he charged her with unfaithfulness to him, a charge that she
speedily denied. She continued to go regularly for wood and water. As the
bear's suspicions continued to exist, he fastened a magic cord to her dress one
of those days, and, following it up, found her in the arms of the hunter.
Hoots, being much enraged, killed the hunter (Touats) after a hard fight.

It is not known whether or not this legend originated in the failure to distinguish between the real bear and the bear totem. It is probable, however,
that the bear totem is referred to. An Indian moralist will find in this story a
warning to wives to be faithful to their husbands.

Above the bear and hunter is "Yalth," or the great raven, carrying in his
beak the new moon and in his claws the dish of fresh water, illustrating the
most familiar version of the Haida legend of the creation. Yalth, the raven
and benefactor of man, stole from his evil uncle, the eagle (the enemy of man),
the new moon which he had imprisoned in a box, and also got fresh water by
strategy from the eagle's daughter. The crafty raven made love to the eagle's
daughter and won her confidence. He then deceived her and flew out through
the smoke hole of the eagle's house, taking the water with him. He also stole
the sun and stars from the boxes in which they were imprisoned by the chief
of tides. When the sun shone forth all the people were frightened and ran in
all directions in search of hiding places. Some flew to the mountains, others
into the sea and many took to the woods.

They were all transformed into animals suited to live in their respective
hiding places. He reached an island in the sea by the help of his magic bird
skin, and seizing a burning brand of fire started on his return to Queen Charlotte island, but the journey was so long that nearly all of the wood burned up,
and even the point of his bill was scorched black, so he had to let it drop.* The
sparks flew in all directions over the whole region, so that ever after both stone
and wood contain fire, which can be obtained from one by striking and from the
other by rubbing. There are many versions of this story of creation, and many
are the adventures of Yalth, the raven, not to mention the other traditions,
which are too numerous for one Indian to learn in a lifetime.

There are several accounts of creation that have gained ground among the
various Haida tribes.

All of them agree that Yalth, or the great raven, is the benefactor of man,
and the creator of all things. According to one of the legends the first people
sprung from a cockle shell, and that the raven stole from the eagle all the
things which were needed by men. According to another tradition the raven
transformed himself into a drop of water and the eagle's daughter having drank
him became impregnated with him and bore him a man child, etc. The Indians

at Houkan have still a different version of the first part of the creation story. According to them the sister of Mughilflass, the first man, was childless, and wished to marry. Her name was Slaugfunt. She sat many days in the house of her brother wishing for a mate to come along and take her. One day she saw a whale-killer pass by, who returned and took her a long way out to sea with him. While gone the man child was born. Varied as these legends are concerning the first part of the creation they all seem to agree that the raven stole the sun, moon and stars from the eagle, and the fresh water from the eagle's daughter, according to the story on the totem column just described, and he did all these criminal deeds for the good of man.

The Haidas show great ingenuity in their carvings on wood, but it is in their slate modelings that their greatest skill is exhibited. They mine their peculiar quality of slate on Queen Charlotte island. When it first comes out of the ground it is soft and easy to work, but after it has been exposed to the atmosphere for a few weeks it becomes very hard and takes a good polish. On this slate they execute work that compares favorably with many of the productions of highly civilized sculptors.

One of their best specimens is the Bear Mother, which also illustrates a legend. There are several versions of it, but here is the most usually accepted:

A number of Indian squaws were in the woods gathering berries when a chief's daughter, who chanced to be among them, ridiculed the whole bear species. The bears poured down upon them and killed all but the chief's daughter, whom the king bear made his wife.

THE BEAR MOTHER

She bore him a child, half human and half bear. She was discovered up a tree one day by a party of Indians, who were out hunting. They mistook her for a bear, but she made them understand that she was human. They took her home and she became the ancestor of all the Indians belonging to the bear totem.

The carving represents the agony of the mother in suckling this rough and uncouth offspring.

The Haidas believe in the transmigration of the soul and that men are merely bears, wolves, ravens and the like transformed into men.

Upon examining their work on silver and copper one will be struck by the neatness of the workmanship as well as the oddness of the designs of the Haida smiths. If the Haida wishes to draw the picture of a man or animal on a bracelet, ring or breast pin, he will split the face in the middle and draw two side views, one facing the other.

HAIDA CHILD DANCE AT HOUKAN

The boxes, food, dishes, implements, in short, everything used by the Haida, are richly carved or painted with the totems of owners, and illustrations of incidents of their lives, or legends of their totems.   On most Haida drawings the eye is placed on the breast, ear, foot, etc., of the figure, to give the idea of general utility of the power of each number to look out for itself. The carved box of black slate shown in the illustration has a sea lion on each end. Each of them has a salmon in its mouth. The face on the side of the box is "Hoots," the brown bear, chewing up the hunter, and represents the same bear and hunter story as has been explained in connection with the totem column in front of the house.

There are many different types of rattles found in that region, the one given in this book being the most common form of shamens or medicine man's rattle. It is carved of the famous yellow cedar wood and painted in several brilliant colors. The carving on the breast represents the sparrow hawk; the tail of the bird is carved to represent another bird's head with a frog in its mouth. The frog is supposed to possess a poison in his head that the medicine man sucks out to give him power to work bad spells.

The figure on the back is Ka-ka-hete, the whistling demon, who lived in the mountains. He was capsized while traveling in his canoe one day and nearly drowned. He swam ashore and made for the woods for shelter. Some times he came down into the villages and stole the children, which he took into the woods with him and ate. In later times he transformed himself into a land otter. The two figures on the top of the rattle tell a story of Haida love-making. The front figure represents the boy, while the other one, the "birdie," if you please, is the girl. The frog passing from one mouth to the other indicates that a lie has been told by one of them, and from the direction that he is traveling it appears that there, as elsewhere, the boy had to bear the blame of it. The rattle, taken as a whole, represents the great raven, with a brand of fire in his mouth, which the Haida nations worship as the creator and benefactor of the human race.

Before the whites came among them the Haidas made knives and daggers of stone and copper, but steel is mostly used among them now-a-days for such purposes. The daggers shown in the illustration have yellow cedar handles, and each has carved on it the individual totems of owner. One of them seems to be a chief of the beaver tribe, and is quite eminent, since there are four disks on his hat.

The Haida tribes are rapidly undergoing a change. They are not slow to abandon their own customs and adopt the methods of the Europeans. If scholars wish to systematically acquaint themselves with the interesting traditions of these people as illustrated by their carving, etching and painting, they would better be about it. Their works are rapidly deteriorating in the face of the new civilization and in the indifference of the present generation. In fact the only young men who now engage in such pursuits are the curi omakers.

CHAPTER XXXIII

Those who have read of the wonderful totemic carvings of the Haidas will no doubt take an interest in the peculiar laws and customs, and the strange moral and esthetical standards of those remarkable people of the North. If judged by the highest standard of nineteenth century civilization, these people would not hold a very high position. But if they were compared to surrounding tribes when they first came in contact with whites, the thing that would be noticed most is the great progress they had themselves made in morals. When first visited by the early explorers these Indians, like all the other Indians on the coast, were bold shameless thieves. With them it was not dishonorable to steal, and, if caught, restitution settled the matter. On the other hand they discriminated between a friend and an enemy and seldom or never, stole from a guest and never robbed one of their own totem or clan. And to this day an unwatched camp or an unlocked house is, with them, sacredly respected, and the most valuable property that is hid in the woods is just as safe from other Indians as if guarded night and day. Unfortunately the white men have set some very bad examples in this respect and the Indians have not so often sinned as they have been sinned against.

In many of their race characteristics social customs, moral standards and traditions, they bear a striking resemblance to the inhabitants of Japan, and Tartary. Like them, they have great respect for the aged, whose advice in most matters has great weight. Some of the older women, even bondwomen in former times, attain great influence in the tribe as soothsayers, due as much to their venerable appearance as to any pretense they may make of working medicine charms. They are remarkably fond of and indulgent to their children, rarely chastising them. Between the sexes the rights of women are respected and the terms of equality on which the men and women live are very striking to most visitors of the region. Although marriage is essentially by purchase, and the question of morality of the wife solely one of sanction by the husband, yet even this restriction is centuries in advance of their Northern neighbors where promiscuity and the most bestial practices prevail. The early voyagers invariably mentioned Haidas as modest and reserved in bearing. The moral virtues of these people have faded considerably in the presence of the new civilization with its artificial needs of finery and luxuries. The vices of civilization have had a most demoralizing effect on the inhabitants of Queen Charlotte and the Prince of Wales islands. Like most savages they are inveterate gamblers and have a strong craving for tobacco and alcohol. In their disregard for the lives of slaves and in their practice of acquitting murderers or other criminals by exacting the payment of indemnity to the relatives of the injured, is seen simply the customs, the operations of which, with them, has the force of law. Murder, seduction, the refusal to marry a widow according to law, causes general war, but any wrong may be righted by the paying of an indemnity of the region. In writing of this subject Sir James Douglas, governor of British Columbia, during the administration of the Hudsons Bay company, says: "If unmarried women prove frail, the partner of their guilt is bound to make reparation to the parents, soothing their wounded honor with handsome presents. A failure to do this would cause the friends of the offending fair one to use force to back up their demands and to revenge the insult. It must not, however, be supposed they would be induced to act this part from any sense of reflected shame, or from any desire of discouraging vice by making a severe example of the vicious, or deem the girl the worse for the accident, or her character in any way blemished. Such are not their feelings, for the offender is simply regarded as a robber who has committed depredations on their merchandise, their only anxiety being to make the damages exacted as heavy as possible."

HAIDA THUNDER-MASK

To such an extent was this question of indemnity carried, that when the Russians tried to interefere with the killing of slaves on ceremonial occasions, they were only successful in preventing it by ransoming the proposed victim. And many were the exactions of the Indians for damages on account of the accidental deaths in the employ of whites.

Along with the other artistic characteristics of these people, they are exceedingly fond of singing and dancing. Some of them have rich voices. Their rude, savage songs are not without melody and many of their weird dances, by the music of various shaped and boistrous drums, exhibit considerable art, especially of imitation. Their imitations of various birds and wild animals, darting in all directions, screaming like seagulls, howling like wolves and screeching like wild geese, imitating the fierce, harsh music of the brown bear, the cries of great eagles and ravens, are all worthy of special mention. They bathe frequently in the sea, but on the other hand, continually daub their faces, bodies and heads with grease and paint. However, this latter custom is largely disappearing except on ceremonial occasions. They were formerly indifferent to the stench of decaying animal matter, but have improved wonderfully in recent years. They are still indifferent to the sanitary laws of ventilation and betray a great fondness for putrid salmon and herring noses, and rancid fish and seal grease. A visit to many of the Haida houses where they have not come to using stoves is still quite a trying ordeal to the uninitiated.

Totemism governs the whole tribal organization of the Indians on Queen Charlotte and the Prince of Wales islands. The ceremonies at birth, initiation, naming, matrimony, feasting, dancing, funerals and all other social occasions, have for their object, in some way, the identity of the phratery, more than of the totem or the carved image of the animal chosen to represent him.

Birth-rights, such as property, rank wealth, etc., are received from the mother. The question as to who is the father of a child is of but little importance. The household is not the unit of the totem or of the phratery, as more than one totem is represented in each, the father belonging to one totem and the mother to another. Besides this, a brother and his wife may belong to the househould, or a sister and her husband; thus numerous totems may be represented under one roof.

In the ordinary sense there is no absolute chieftainship. The family is the political unit. The richest head of a household or the one who has the greatest number of influential relations predominates over the rest and is nominally the chief of the village. His authority is shadowy and is dependent largely, aside from wealth and family influence, on personal prowess in time of war, or on an aggressive personality. In short the prominence of the chief is all that he can make it by the arts of assertion, bargain, intrigue, wealth, display and personal prowess. There are also petty chiefs who represent the principal clan totems or households. For each household is with them a subordinate government. The head chief merely overshadows in the extent of his influence, the petty chiefs. Often reverses of fortune turns the tables so that some decline in influence, while others rise in importance. Often the medicine men or shamens unite with the chiefs to strengthen each other in the fear and respect of the people. And bitter are many of the feuds arising from the rivalries of households struggling for power in the tribe.

As a rule a chief is not treated with any marked deference except upon ceremonial occasions when many marks of respect are shown him. When engaged in treaty-making it is common to see him carried on the shoulders of his attendants, as well as being made the central figure of many pompous ceremonies. Slavery was common among them up to the acquisition of Alaska by the

United States government in 1867. The slaves did all the drudgery, fished and hunted for their master; and strengthened his forces in time of war. When they were too old to work they were for the most part killed and many of them were sacrificed on ceremonial occasions. They were never allowed to marry or hold property.

Councils were usually called only on occasions or necessity, there being no stated period for them. Women usually had as much to say in these meetings as men, especially on questions of trade, when their advice was always given whether it was sought or not. However, they usually kept mum on ceremonial occasions. In these deliberative bodies they sit in a squatting position with legs crossed and deliver formal speeches in turn which are heard with wrapt attention and approved by grunts and various other signs.

In the division of labor men and women are quite nearly equal among the Haidas. The men are the warriors and hunters although a women of rank generally steers the war canoe. The different kinds of work are usually divided among the people according to their skill. Some are exclusively implement makers, others are wood carvers, and many of the women follow basket making as a trade. Every chief keeps a man employed constantly as a canoe maker. A visitor to a Haida camp will be struck with the apparent equality of the sexes. The woman is always free with advice, and a distinguished traveler has said cases of " hen-pecked " husbands are not rare.

Very peculiar laws of inheritance and relationship exist among the Haida people. First cousins may marry, but totally unrelated persons of the same phratery cannot. In wars between households a groom may be called upon to bear arms against his father-in-law on account of some feud of trifling importance. Poligamy is tolerated but seldom practiced.

Property is inherited by the brother of the deceased, a brother's son, a sister's son, or the mother in the order named in the absence of the preceding one. As a rule the wife gets nothing but her own dowry. Whoever inherits the property, if he be a brother or a brother's or sister's son, must either marry the widow or pay an indemnity to her relatives. In case the heir is already married, the next in succession takes her; for instance, the brother may inherit the property and the nephew get the widow. It will be observed that by the laws and customs of the Haidas, they not only prevent the accumulation of wealth and power in one branch of a family and allow it to grow opulent, corrupt and rotten, but provide for the widows as well. It is the duty of the heir within a year after the cremation or burial of the deceased to erect a commemorative column at the grave or elsewhere in honor of him. It usually contains his crest or sub-totem at the top and recites some of the leading incidents of his life. Among the Haidas conjugal virtues have only a commercial value. They are something to be bought and sold. One Haida thinks nothing of selling his

wife to another provided he can get his price.   And cases of one Indian renting
his wife to another are very common.

Mr. McLeod tells the story of a case of this kind shortly after the establishment of a justice court at Houkan.   It was, by the way, the first case that was
called for trial in said court.   One Indian was quite deeply indebted to the other,
so in order to satisfy the debt he rented his wife to his creditor for a couple of
weeks.   At the expiration of the appointed time the Indian refused to return
the wife to her rightful owner, and the injured husband appealed to the strong
arm of American law to recover his property.

Tatooing on the breast and arms of Haidas is quite general.   They are
usually representations of some totem and commemorate deeds and adventures
of their lives.   The women usually wear earrings and bracelets, and rings are
often worn through the noses of chiefs.

Although the methods of sepulture have changed in recent years, the ceremonies remain much as they formerly were.   On the demise of an important
personage it is customary to array the body in ceremonial apparel and surround
it with the tokens of his or her wealth.   Thus laid out in state the relatives and
friends view the remains.   In case that it is a great chief who is well-known,
Indians come from other villages, and the body is thus displayed until in an advanced stage of decomposition, when the final rites take place.   In former times
many of the slaves of the deceased were dispatched at the funeral.   During the
first day's ceremonines the body was borne to the pyre, which had been constructed in the rear of some house formerly owned by the deceased, and reduced
to ashes.   In the meantime the mourners gathered themselves around the pyre
and with painted faces, their hair cut short, and their heads sprinkled with
eagles' down they bewailed in the most dismal manner, the loss of their kinsman.   The service usually closes with a feast.   The ashes were preserved and
deposited in a box near the top of the commemorative column erected in honor
of the deceased.   In recent times the burial custom has taken the place of cremation.

The houses of the Haidas are remarkable for their strength and comfort.
Their frame consists of huge logs, often two or more feet in diameter, as posts
planted securely in the ground, and large log plates of equal proportions resting on them.   The remainder of the frame is heavy and strong in proportion.
The posts are so beveled in the sides that they hold the hewn planks in position, that compose the wall, while those that constitute the roof are held in
place by the weight of rocks.   The smoke holes are so arranged that protection
can readily be shifted from one side to the other so that the wind won't blow
down through it.   The dimensions of these houses are often 18x20 feet, and 12
or 15 feet high.   The various timbers are placed in position by the aid of rope
guys.   The work of building a house often extends over a period of several

years, as most of the timbers are very heavy to handle by hand and must be carved before being placed in position.   Great crowds are employed in building these houses and great festivities are indulged in on the days occupied in the raising of the huge timber into position, corresponding to our lifting-bees, so common in the rural districts.   The houses are generally made of Sitka spruce and yellow cedar wood.

The great totem columns in front of the houses are usually upwards of two feet in diameter and vary considerably in height.   They are for the most part carved out of yellow cedar wood by the native artist employed for the occasion to commemorate the great achievements of the wealthy house-holder, to celebrate the glory of his ancestors and record the more interesting traditions of his totem.

These columns are never taken down or removed, but are allowed to stand until, in many places, only the decayed stump remains.   In Houkan large numbers of totem columns are standing where the houses have long since fallen down and many of them will be found in dense thickets.   There is one in front of the residence of Rev. J. L. Gould that has quite a spruce tree growing in the top of it.   The tall columns shown in the illustration, in front of the houses, record the adventures, genealogy and legends of the owner, and his totem.   The shorter ones at the corners of the houses, and in grave yards, are commemorative columns erected in honor of a former occupant of the house.

No one is allowed to execute these carvings among the Haidas until he has first had the medicine inoculated into his fingers by the shamens.

SKAMSON THE THUNDERER—HAI-
DA TATOOING

CORNER OF THE VILLAGE OF HOUKAN

CHAPTER XXXIV

MYTHOLOGY AND NATIVE HISTORY

The column with the great heads on top, shown in the illustration, tells quite an interesting story. It is variously told in different localities, however, the versions differ only in the minor details.

The top group represents the head of an European with whitened face and long black beard, flanked on either side by children wearing tall hats, and represents the following legend:

A very long time ago a chief's wife left the temporary camp used by the Indians during the summer season, and taking her two small children with her she went in a small fishing canoe across the narrows to get some spruce boughs on which salmon eggs could be collected. She drew up her canoe on the beach and warned her children not to wander off. On her return nothing was seen of the children, they having disappeared. Many times she called to them, and they always answered her from the woods with voices of crows. Always when she sought them, two crows mocked her from the trees. The children never returned and it was said that a white trader kidnaped them and carried them off in his ship. The face with the beard represents the European, and the figures on either side are the kidnaped children which he is taking away with him.

Whether or not this story was founded on facts cannot be learned definitely. However, some form of it is found in nearly every Haida village, and as a nursery tale to frighten refractory children it is a great favorite.

Next proceeding down the column is Hootzy, the wolf, and the children, and below it is the mother bent over and weeping bitterly. The woman, Kitsinao, of the crow totem, had many children and was very proud of them (many with the Haida means more than four). She scoffed at the woman of the wolf totem who had but one puny child. The feelings of the woman were wounded so she appealed to her totem for protection and aid. A band of huge Siberian wolves at once descended from the woods that line the borders of those great hills and killed all of the sons and daughters of the crow mother. The mother was very sad and sat down on a rock and wept bitterly all the days of her life. In time she became incorporated with it and to this day a traveler on the Prince of Wales island who chances to call into American bay will see this modern Niobe bent over and weeping bitterly. The Haida asks no questions as to the authenticity of these stories, the fact that they have been carved on wood and slate, and that the said rock is in existence is conclusive proof to him.

Next comes the story of the seagull, the beaver, and the beaver's daughter.

At one time there lived on the solitary shore of Daal island a beaver with his only daughter, Cawk. His wife had long been dead and the two had led a quiet life together. Cawk grew to be a handsome girl and all the youths or Houkan, as well as others from far and near came to sue for her hand, but none of them could touch her proud heart. Finally, at the thawing of the snow in the spring, a great seagull flew over the sea to the beaver's house and wooed Miss Calk with his enticing song:

> Come to me! Come into the land of the birds where there is never hunger,
> Where my house is made of the most beautiful woods,
> You shall rest on soft bear skins.
> My companions, the gulls, shall bring you food.
> Their feathers shall clothe you,
> Your fire shall always be supplied with fuel.
> Your basket shall always be filled with meat.

HAIDA GRAVE YARD—SHOWING TOTEM OF DEAD

Cawk could not long resist such wooing and they went together over the vast sea. When at last they reached the country in which the gull had his home, Cawk discovered that her spouse had shamefully deceived her. Her new home was not built of beautiful woods, but was only a tent of fish skins, which were full of holes. It was a most wretched place that gave free entrance to wind and snow. Instead of soft bear skins, her bed was made of miserable hard hair-seal hides, and her only food was the disgusting, half rotten fish which the birds brought her. Too soon she discovered that she had thrown away her opportunities when, in her foolish pride, she had rejected the Houkan youth. In her woe she sang:

> Sung! Oh, Father:
> If you knew how wretched I am you would come to me and we would hurry
>   away in your canoe over the waters.
> The birds look unkindly upon a stranger in their camp.
> Cold winds roar about my bed.
> They give me miserable food.
> Oh, come father, and take me home again.

When a year was passed all the sea was again stirred by warmer winds, the father left his home opposite Houkan to visit his daughter Cawk. His daughter greeted him joyfully and begged of him to take her back home. The father hearing of the outrages wrought upon his daughter determined upon revenge. He killed the gull, took Cawk into his canoe and quickly left the country which had brought so much sorrow to the daughter. When the other gulls came home and found their companion dead and his wife gone, they all flew away in search of the fugitives. They were very sad over the death of their poor murdered comrade and continue to mourn and cry until this day.

Having flown a short distance they saw the canoe and stirred up a heavy storm. The sea rose in immense waves and threatened the pair with destruction. In this mortal peril the selfish father determined to offer Cawk to the birds and flung her overboard. She clung to the edge of the canoe with a death grip. The cruel father then took a knife and cut off the joints of her fingers. The joint of the first finger falling into the sea was transformed into a whale, and the nail became whale bone. The joints of the second finger became grampuses, or killers, while the nail was transformed into those great fins which are so conspicuous in the Haida's representation of the killer. The remainder of the joints swam away as salmon, herring, codfish, sea otters, hair seals, and fur seals. In the meantime the storm had abated for the gulls thought Cawk was drowned. The father then allowed her to come into the boat again. But from that time she cherished a deadly hatred against him and swore bitter revenge. After they got ashore she called her totem guardians, the wolves, and let them gnaw off the feet and hands of her father, while he was asleep. Upon waking the beaver cursed himself, his daughter and the wolves which had thus crippled him; whereupon the earth opened and swallowed the hut, the father, the daughter and the wolves.

Upon the whole, the column just described may be said to be purely legendary, yet it seems quite generally to refer to the wolf totem.

In front of the residence of Chief Schooltka is also a column that is full of interest. It was erected by himself and the carvings were executed with steel instruments, so that superior designs and neater workmanship have been obtained.

At the top of it is his crest or sub-totem, the eagle. The various carvings trace in a general way the history of family for several generations back, such as marriages of one totem with another. For instance, the bear to the eagle, the wolf to the raven, etc. It also indicates the number of children in each family, and the manner of death that ended their lives by some conventional means that is readily understood by the Haida. About midway down the pole is a rude representation of a Russian priest of the Greek church with his hands folded across his breast in reverential manner, with crude images of angels around him and beneath it is the only legend carved on the column, it is the bear and butterfly story, which is worth repeating:

CHAPTER XXXV

In the beginning, when Yalth, the great raven, the friend and benefactor of the human race, was looking for a good region for men to occupy, the butterfly hovered over his head as he flew. When he came to the country now occupied by the Haida nations, the butterfly pointed with his proboscis to the good lands and said, "Where the bear are, there salmon, sprouts and good living will be found in abundance;" so that accounts for the residence of the Haidas on the Prince of Wales island, and for bear living so plentifully in that region.

At the base of the column is the beaver, the totem of Schooltka's wife and children.

At one corner of his house is a commemorative column somewhat shorter than the totem column erected to his memory. Among other events pictured on the incompleted column is his cordial welcome to the missionary and the children with books in their hands, illustrate quite truthfully the attitude toward the whites of this most truly noble Indian of the Haida race. He was always the friend of the white man, and when the Rev. J. L. Gould, the Presbyterian missionary arrived in the village, he received a warm welcome from Schooltka. His comfortable house was placed at the disposal of the missionary and his family, and the mission school was conducted there for several years. The chief has now been dead several years, but leaves a wife who possesses many of his good qualities and shares in his friendship for the whites.

A visit to the home of Mrs. Schooltka would not be without interest. The house is a modern form of Haida dwelling, covering quite an extensive area and two stories in height, but constructed of huge timbers and hewed boards in Haida fashion. One wishing to enter is conducted down several steps to the door, which opens on the first floor, which is several feet below the level of the ground. One large room includes all the lower portion of the house. The great posts which compose its massive frame are richly carved and painted with various traditions of the race, tribe and family. Slate and wood carving rattles, carved instruments, models of various shaped canoes and soldier clothes are scattered hither and thither. There is a stage-like platform about six feet in width reaching quite around a room which is only partially lighted by two windows in the front of the house. In the center of the room a large box stove has taken the place of the crude fireplace and smoke hole of their more savage days. In one corner is a modern cooking stove with its pots, kettles, pans, skillets, etc., showing that civilized methods of cooking have superceded the old way of cooking meat and fish on sticks, or by roasting in holes dug in the ground under a hot fire. Mrs. Schooltka has found an easier way of boiling her food than by putting it in a water-tight basket, covering it with water and casting hot stones into it. But after all the most strikingly interesting figure in the room is Mrs. Schooltka herself. In stature she is short and stout, though her figure is by no means repulsive. She possesses a very alert expression of countenance and her face is on the whole pleasing. Though about 40 years of age, one would think her very much younger, owing to the absence of wrinkles in her face. She takes a keen interest in everything, and never tires of telling stories of her late husband. A visitor would no doubt be much amused at the very indefinite idea of time which these Indians have. Thus, if this good, but simple-minded woman is asked how long she lived with her husband, her answer will be, in mixed English and Chinook, " Klo-nass, ni-ka ha-lo, cum-tux; nika tum-tum klone hundred years," mean-

MRS. SCHOOLTKA, WHO LIVED 300 YEARS WITH HER HUSBAND

ing that she was not sure, but thought she had lived with him about 300 years.

There is one thing in which the Haidas differ widely from other Indians: they are not fond of bright colors in their clothing, black being always preferred. Even in their shawls and handkerchiefs they prefer that they be black or some other conservative color. Missionary societies sending them second-handed clothing make a great mistake in this particular.

Though the Haidas are as fond of display as formerly their ceremonial dances, in which the whole tribe engaged, are now rare, in fact they have not been seen for several years. The spirit of imitation has taken hold of the Haida and he now copies the methods of Europeans in such matters. Most of the petty chiefs have been to Victoria, B. C., and seen the soldiers drill. They have also witnessed the operations of the fire department of that place.

Copying British styles they have uniformed themselves with red coats, forming quite a large army, and have a brilliantly uniformed fire company. Their parades are frequent and they present a very self-important, if not formidable, appearance as they march proudly along, keeping time to the wild, grand music of the tribes, their own boisterous drums, and the native whistles and trumpets, through their rough narrow streets, performing various evolutions and halting to drill. Indifferent whether armed with guns or sticks, many of the swords of the officers being of wood, they draw up in line, go through the facings, marching and counter-marching, the manual of arms and various other exercises. Conspicuous on such occasions is Mr. John, whose portrait is here presented. He is very ambitious to become one of the general officers of the army. So, as often as the drilling day comes around he calls on the Rev. Gould, who was a soldier in the late civil war, for instructions in military tactics. On one occasion the good man asked him if he expected to learn in a moment what it took him (Mr. Gould) three years to learn. This discouraged Mr. John for a time, but he soon recovered and is now occasionally a military pupil of Mr. Gould's. The parades of the fire company are pompous and magnificent, but damaging stories are told of them so far as their real usefulness is con-

SILVER AND COPPER ORNAMENTS
HAIDA INDIANS

cerned. One evening Mr. E. T. McLeod looked out of the door of his store and beheld one of the Indian's houses in flames. With the aid of a fire extinguisher and a little water he quickly quenched the blaze before the fire company arrived. The Indians who composed the company were very angry with him for not waiting until they could get their suits on and reach the scene in dress parade uniform. The latter incident illustrates the childish notions of a savage race capable of a high degree of cultivation.

CHAPTER XXXVI

POTLATCH AND DEVIL DANCE

The potlatch was the greatest institution of the Indian, and is to this day. It was the crowning glory of the Indian life and worth the meade of a thousand victories over the foe. It was the ambition of the hyas tyee, the politics of every ruler who could secure wealth enough to accomplish the great and glorious end. It impoverished the giver but brought gladness to the hearts of the people, and honor ever after to him who gave. It was a beautiful custom; beautiful in the eyes of the natives of high or low degree, confined to no particular tribe but to be met with everywhere along the coast. It no doubt had its origin far back in the misty past. Come from whence — who can tell? Perhaps, through the generations of the world down through all the ups and downs and changes and variation of mankind, keeping step with that most beautiful of all civilized customs, the gifts of Yuletide, for Christ's sake, and perchance the very same origin marked the beginning of both.

Before the introduction of the cloths and implements of civilized man, the simple native satisfied himself and the people by giving of those things he could gather from the chase or manufacture by his crude arts. Skins of wild animals fancifully wrought and colored, the wild ponies of his herds, bows and arrows, his canoes, everything he sacrificed on the altar of the potlatch which meant a gift, to give, etc. When he was enabled to get blankets, knives, guns, etc., from the whites the potlatch took a wider range and not even the glittering yellow gold was spared the sacrifice. The great day set so many suns or moons ahead, arrived, great was the interest and excitement of the occasion. From far and near assembled the invited guests and tribes and with feasting, singing, chanting and dancing, the bounteous collection was distributed; a chief was made penniless, the wealth of a life time was dissipated in an hour, but his head forever after was crowned with the glory of a satisfied ambition; he had won the honor and reverence of the people.

The gifts were not always preserved by the recipients, especially with some of the Sound tribes for it was a work of a noble unselfish brave to immediately destroy whatever had been thrown to him. So it was that fine new blankets, guns, bows and arrows and the like were often destroyed scarcely before they touched the ground. At the Old-Man-House potlatches have been given within the residency of the whites when the frenzied Indians have fallen upon a shower of gifts and soon had them entirely destroyed. The blankets, easily secured by barter with the Hudsons Bay company's agents, were usually hung up and with knives and daggers would in a twinkling be slashed and cut into hundreds of fragments and strips. The blankets in those days cost a great deal of money, $10 to $20 a pair, so that in a very short time hundreds of dollars worth of valuables would soon be destroyed.

Back in the distant past and not within the memory of the Indians of to-day the ceremony had its attendant features of a more heathenish kind, for the blood of sacrifice was spilled as a more fitting observance of the grand occasion. Slaves succumbed to the horrible rites and moaned out their death chants which blended and contrasted with the mirthful song of their possessors, engaged for the time in their dance of blood. An incident of the awful tragedies is inspiringly told, if such a construction can be put upon it, by an early missionary, an eye witness, whose description is re-clothed in the splendid words of Hezzekiah Butterworth:

"I once witnessed a potlatch and I hope I may never see such a scene again. I had landed among a tribe of northern Indians on the Whulge, where I had gathered a little church some months before, and I expected to hold a meeting on the night I arrived in one of the canoes. The place was deserted; the woods were all silent. Sunset flashed his red light along the sea, such a sunset as one only sees here in these northern latitudes. A wannish glare of smoky crimson lingering long into the night. As soon as the sun went down I began to hear a piping sound like birds in all the woods around. The calls answered one another everywhere. I had never heard a sound like that. I tried to approach one of the sounds but it receded before me.

"Suddenly a great fire blazed up and lit the sky. I approached it; it was built on a little prairie. Near it was a large platform covered with canoes, blankets, pressed fish, berry cakes, soap — clayey or berry soap, wampum and beads. Not an Indian was in sight save one. She was an old squaw bound to a stake or tree.

" ' What is this?' I asked in Chinook.
" ' Cultus tee-hee.'
" ' Cultus tee-hee?'
" ' Dah-blo!'
" She wailed in Chinook.
" ' When — tamala?' (to-morrow.)
" ' Ding Ding '—
" ' Cultus tee-hee.'
" ' Cultus hee-hee.'
" ' Dah-blo!'

"Then I knew that all was preparation for a potlatch, and that there was to be a devil dance — ding ding — at that very hour.

"It was a night of the full moon, as such a night would be selected for such a ceremony. The moon rose red in the smoky air, and the sounds like the bird calls grew louder and wilder. Then there was a yell; it was answered everywhere, and hundreds of Indians in paint and masks came running out of the timber upon the prairie. Some were on all fours, some had the heads of beasts, fishes and birds, some had wings and many tails.

"Then came biters attended by raving squaws. The biters were to tear the flesh from the arms of any who were not found at the dance after a certain hour.

"Now the drums began to beat and the shells to blow. Indians poured out of the woods in paint, blankets and beads.

A great circle dance was formed; the ta-mahn-a-wis or spirit dance was enacted. Great gifts were made as at a pow-wow or wah-wah. Then the dark crowd grew frantic, and under the full moon gleaming on high came the devil's dance.

"The first victim was a live dog. He was seized, torn in pieces and eaten by the dancers, so as to redden their faces with blood. The yells were now more furious; the dancers leaped into the air and circled around the old woman tied to the tree.

"I will not describe the sickening sight that followed; I will only say that the old hag, who was accused of casting an evil eye, shared the same fate as the dog.

"'Why do you worship the devil?' I asked an exhausted brave the next day.

"'Good spirits always good; him we no fear. Please the devil and him no harm you. All well — happy; good ta-mahn-a-wis, bad ta-mahn-a-wis, see?'

QUINIAULT TRIBESMAN

It was plain — the old philosophy of the sinking sailor who prayed 'good lord! good devil!' The tradition was — it came out of the long past — that the devil must be appeased.

CHAPTER XXXVII

THE T'KLINKITS AND ALEUTS

The T'Klinkit is the name applied to all the Indians on the upper coast who reside between the north end of Prince of Wales island and Yakutat bay, near the base of Mt. St. Elias.

These T'Klinkits are divided into so-called tribes; virtually families, the chieftainship descending through the female line. The T'Klinkits were generally known to the Siwash of Puget Sound under the general name of Stickeens.

Among the principal families of T'Klinkits are the Stickeens, located on the Stikeen river, which is near Fort Wrangle; the Takous and Aukos, whose head-quarters are in Takou inlet and on the present site of Juneau; the Chilkats and Chilkoots, at the present head of navigation near Pyramid harbor; the Hoon-yas, near Glacier bay, and the Hootzenoos, near the present town of Killisnoo, and the Sitkas, on Baranoff island. The Sitkas are really composed of two families — the Kaksutis and the Kokwautans.

In 1858 Commander Meade, U. S. N., found it necessary to reduce to ashes two villages of the Kake Indians on Kiou island, on account of the murder of innocent prospectors. These Kake Indians are the most hostile of any of the Alaska families. They are probably not T'Klinkits. It has been urged by some that they, as well as the Haidas, just to the south of them, are descendants of the ancient Aztecs of Mexico, who were driven out upon the fall of the great Montezuma.

Later outbreaks occurred among the northern Indians as late as 1879. The garrison at Sitka, which had been established in 1877, had been withdrawn, and Catlian, chief of the Kaksutis, had an idea, and so informed all the T'Klinkits, that the United States had abandoned the country; the natives were sole owners, and all persons in the country were there at their peril. He first started off making orations at Sitka, where he stirred up the young men of his family to attempt the massacre of all the residents of Sitka, telling his friends that "they could kill everybody, loot the stores, secure enough to keep them several years, take to the mountains, and in a year or so all would be forgotten by the United States government." Luckily for the people of Sitka, Annahootz, the chief of the Kokwautans, learned of Catlian's threats, and one evening when a crowd of drunken Kaksutis attempted to pass the stockade between what is called Indian Town and Sitka, Annahootz, with several of his young, men met them at the gate. A skirmish took place. Annahootz was badly wounded, but prevented Catlian's crowd from reaching the citizens.

The then collector of customs, Col. M. D. Ball, as far as possible armed the citizens, who patroled the town night and day until the arrival of the mail steamer from the Sound. An urgent request was forwarded the government for help, and help was also asked from the British government at Victoria. The American government being dilatory, Capt. A'Court, of H. M. S. Osprey, went immediately to the scene of trouble. Through the urgent representations of Major Wm. Gouveneur Morris, at that time special agent of the treasury de-

YAKUTAT, ALASKA

partment (afterwards collector of customs for Alaska), the revenue marine steamer Wolcott was immediately sent north. As soon as orders could be given, the United States corvette Alaska was sent to Sitka. Upon the arrival of the Wolcott, Capt. A'Court offered the hospitalities of his cabin to Mrs. Ball and family to convey them from the scene of trouble. Col. Ball thought he, with the assistance of the Wolcott and Alaska, could hold the natives in shape, and declined the offer. The trouble blew over, as Catlian saw he was over-matched. The Alaska sailed south, and trouble again being threatened the Jamestown was ordered to that port. Under the wise regulations of Captains Beardsley and Glass, Indian Town (so called) was cleansed, whitewashed, the turbulent natives being made policemen and carried on the rolls of the ship as landsmen. They liked their authority, and with their big tin stars, brass buttons and blue uniforms kept the place in good order.

The only other trouble was in 1883, at the Hootzenoo village uprising, when Capt. Merriman, of the navy, was forced to destroy the villiage, for which he was afterwards court-martialed and acquitted.

The Chilkats and Kakes have, up to this time, had the reputations of being the worst in Alaska.

Of the T'Klinkits and their peculiar customs and changed conditions at the present day, the *Alaska Searchlight* in March last had the following to say:

"Inter-tribal wars among the natives of southeastern Alaska have become things of the past. A century's contact with the whites has made the T'Klinkits a changed people, differing in exact ratio as that association has been the more or less intimate. Gone forever are their most striking characteristics, their native customs and institutions, until today their warlike achievements live only in song and story. Shamenism, witchcraft and slavery have disappeared before the growing power of the white man as the dreams of night are chased away by the morning sun; but as in bosky dell or depth of woodland shade the dewy shadows linger longest, so traces of former customs still remain among those natives farthest removed from the white man's influence. Fierce and bloody were the frequent wars waged among the different tribes before they felt the rule of the Russians, who did all in their power to divert the attention of the Indians from warfare to the less dangerous pursuit of hunting, Gradually they caught the spirit of trade which actuated their new and powerful neighbors, and adapted new methods for the settlement of their fueds and differences. In time blankets and other articles of value came to be received in payment for insulted dignity or outraged honor, for which formerly no atonement was known save that of blood. Captives of war became slaves to their captors and passed their lives in bondage, unless fortune chanced to smile upon the standards of their people and they were retaken by them. The T'Klinkits waged war upon the British Columbia Indians and took from them many prisoners. At times the most warlike tribes held a considerable number of slaves, but as marriages among them were of rare occurrence, and their number depleted by sacrifice, when the wars ceased, thus cutting off the source of supply, slavery soon died out, until at the present time there are no slaves left. An old doctor at the village on the Takou river has a man with him who is said to be a slave, but he has so many opportunities to escape and implore the protection of the law that either he must be free or does not find his bondage irksome. Kuh-hahla-tloo-ut was formerly a slave. Her face is an exceedingly good type of the old T'Klinkit women, who have learned patience and submission through long years of toil and hardship. Report has it that there is one slave at the Chilkat village of Klak-wan, but practically he is free, although at one time he was owned by a former chief. Under the Russian rule wars among the T'Klinkit tribes became of rare occurrence, but the number of slaves was kept up by purchase from the Indians of British Columbia, chiefly the Flatheads. Throughout the history of the world in all climes and under all conditions slavery has presented the same general characteristics, and among the T'Klinkits there was no exception to the rule. Slaves had no civil rights whatever. They could own no property; whatever came to them through labor or gift belonged to the master. They could not marry without his consent, which was rarely ever given. When liberated, as they sometimes were, they ranked the lowest among the people and were counted with their mother's clan. On festive occasions they were often killed or set free. At the death of a chief or head man it was customary to kill one or more slaves, sometimes ten or fifteen, that they might accompany their master and serve him in the life beyond this earthly existence. The killing of these slaves was attended with but little pomp or ceremony, their death was the one thing to be accomplished. Among the Chilkats, it would be decided in a secret council which of the slaves should be put to

VOLCANO BOGUSLOF, OF ALEUTIAN ISLANDS

death. Unconscious of their impending doom they would be struck down from behind with a huge stone hammer. Able-bodied slaves were seldom sacrificed, as they were considered of too much value, but the old and diseased were usually selected as victims. If a slave should learn of his doom and succeed in escaping or concealing himself he was allowed to live, and after the festivities were over might return to the house of his master with no fear of punishment. Chiefs often used to help favorite slaves make their escape. After death the body of a slave received no more honor than that of a dog. It was denied the right of cremation and thrown upon the beach, food for the wolves, the fish and the birds. On the last evening of great feasts the host would retire to a corner of the house accompanied by all his slaves and don his finest costume — one kept especially for such occasions. His favorite slave would be called upon to dress him, and would receive for his services his freedom. One or more of the others

would be put to death, and after the sacrifice the valor of the chief and his ancestors would be sung, and a distribution of gifts take place. Sometimes a host
would present guests whom he wished to honor greatly with one or more slaves.
At the potlatch at Klakwan last fall the wolf robe of the chief was taken from
its hiding place and shown the people, and no blood sacrifice demanded, though
the last time their eyes rested upon this much-prized relic it is said that six
slaves were killed to do honor to the host."

On the Aleutian islands, or peninsula of Alaska, are found the Aleuts, still
presided over by priests and bishops of the Greek church. It is probable that
no thoroughbred Aleuts now remain in the territory. The present inhabitants
of the Aleutian isles all contain Russian blood in their veins. The mixture has
improved them much, in appearance at least. Formerly they were of diminutive stature, not unlike the Eskimo in their appearance and in the treachery of
their disposition. Now they are much larger in size, and it would be difficult
to distinguish many of them from Europeans, so fair is their complexion and
regular their features. The children, who attend the government schools, learn
everything easily, except mathematics. They very rarely pass fractions in the
arithmetic. Many of them sing hymns and patriotic songs well, and use the English language very fluently when at play. Apparently all are devout Chris-
tians according to the Greek faith, but the sailor who goes ashore at night will
be accosted many times by the Aleuts, both men and women, who want "huchi-
noo," or whisky as we would call it. Cattle, sheep and goats are raised to a
considerable extent around Unalaska. Several fine appearing Jersey and Guern-
sey cows were seen there with their udders well filled with milk. The Aleuts
ride from place to place in bidarkees, or skin canoes. About Dutch harbor are cen-
ters interesting for the tribe, and churchs and schools are maintained. The services
are largely attended by the Aleut portion of Unalaska's population. There are a
bishop and several priests present, who chant the service in Slavonian, wihch is
responded to by a small choir consisting for the most part of young boys. Vast
sums are lavished on the ornamentation of Greek churches. Many are the designs in gold and silver on the furniture used in the service. Like in the ancient
Roman churches the services are conducted by the light of many brilliant can-
dles of various size. Some of the paintings that ornamented the Alaskan Greek
churches, especially those of Sitka and Kodiak, are among the finest artistic
productions of the Slavonian school. While the dignitaries are chanting the
service the greater portion of the congregation keep constantly in motion, kneel-
ing and bowing their heads, and kissing the floor and crossing themselves in
Grecian fashion.

The Grecian cross differs materially from the Roman cross. The Roman
cross is but one erect cross. The upright portion of the Greek cross is crossed
three times, once by a horizontal bar and twice by inclined cross bars, one being

above and the other below the horizontal bar. These crosses are to be found on all their churches and in all their cemeteries.

Dutch harbor is the headquarters of the North American Commercial company for the northern district, and contains such buildings as are usual in a station of its importance. It is the outfitting point for most whalers and sealers for Bering sea, and is the place where American war vessels receive their supply of coal, which is imported from Nanaimo, B. C. The harbor is one of those small bays, well protected by the steep, high hills which surround it, that are so common in Alaska.

Unalaska proper is about a mile and a half away — situated on a long, low flat under the shadow of several lofty hills. Its harbor is as safe as Dutch harbor, but not so handy. The Alaska Commercial company has a large establishment there. The town consists chiefly of the company's large buildings

KODIAK, ALASKA

and about a hundred or more small tenement houses that the company has erected for the use of its native hunters. All the houses are built of imported rustic, and in most cases are painted with brown ocher. The old Greek church has been demolished to give place to a grand new cathedral, which is now under construction. At the present time the devotees meet to burn their incense and otherwise worship in one of the smaller ecclesiastical buildings.

The Alaska Commercial company has secured passage of a special law allowing the natives of Unalaska to hunt sea otters at sea on schooners fitted out in Unalaska, a privilege that none other than they enjoy.

The readers of accounts of adventures on northern seas and frigid lands, such as often appear in magazines and story books, are apt to confound the fur seal, hunted for that rich under fur which he possesses, with the hair seal hunted by the natives of northern regions for the most part for his fat. However, the skins of the latter are of considerable value to a savage man. In the Aluetian islands their bidarkees (skin canoes), houses, clothing, etc., are largely made from the skin of the hair seal. It has not been uncommon in recent years to see in the great illustrated monthlies and weeklies pictures and descriptions of Greenland Eskimos and Siberian Tungusees stealing upon the inoffensive seal as he lies sleeping on a block of ice, with their short spears and other weapons used in his capture. Though so much has been written about hair seals, but very little has appeared in popular publications concerning the more valuable fur seal. This is largely due to the difficulty of obtaining correct information concerning them. In former times they inhabited the northern and southern parts of the Atlantic and Pacific oceans. But they have been so closely hunted that at the present time the only rookeries left that are worthy of mention are those on the Pribylof islands, of which St. Paul and St. George are the chief, the Copper island rookeries along the coast of Siberia and those in the waters of Japan. There are also rookeries in the southern seas, along the coast of Patagonia, but the seals are not very plentiful, and owing to the inclemency of the weather can only be obtained by raiding the rookeries.

In order that the process of hunting the fur seal may be better understood it may be proper to give a little space to a description of them and their habits. They are usually brown or gray in color. The males reach maturity when about ten years old. They often measure eight feet from the nose to the end of the flipper, and their weight often approaches 400 pounds. Some of them live to a great age and have fine long manes on their necks. The females arrive at maturity when about three years old, and vary in weight from 40 to 100 pounds. The male seals are all congregated on the rookery in the latter part of June. The females arrive there several weeks later. As fast as the females arrive the strong old patriarchs take them in charge, each caring for as many as he can guard, usually about fifteen in number. Very soon after the female reaches the island the young one, usually known as the "pup," is born. At birth it weighs only a couple of pounds, and grows to weigh 25 or 30 pounds during the first year. It is said the noise of fierce fighting among the many thousands male seals that gather on these wild, barren, rocky shores at breeding time is beyond the power of human speech to describe. Many thousands of them are killed every year, so fierce are their raging battles. Strange as it may seem, in most cases the young pups do not take readily to the water at first. More often than not the older ones have to teach them how to swim.

As soon as the pups can travel the herds leave the rookery and proceed southward. They go through passes that separate the Aleution islands one from the other in the latter part of September. The 1st of November finds them drifting around in their winter quarters off the coast of Mexico. As soon as good weather returns they proceed northward slowly, congregating along the various fishing banks, where they are most successfully hunted.

The country on the main land, both on the Shumagin islands and the Alaska peninsula as well as on the Aleutian chain, is composed of ragged bluffs and deep canyons, betraying evidence of much volcanic activity in recent times. Where the rocks do not come to the surface these hills are generally covered by a thin growth of small alders which rarely grow to be more than six or seven feet in height. Between the clusters of alder there are often found growing salmon-berry bushes which seldom exceed a foot in height. Grass sprinkled with fragrant violets, grows luxuriantly in some places. In others wild strawberries and small blackberry vines are abundant.

In those latitudes strawberries and salmon-berries are ripe in the middle of August; red and black huckleberries and blackberries in the latter part of September. It is one of the few places where a cranberry marsh can be found on a steeply sloping hillside.

Sand Point station contains a store with warehouses, and customs house and such other buildings as are usually found in a frontier trading post. There is also a large hotel which was built during the administration of Mr. O'Bryon as factor for Lynde & Hough. O'Bryon has since been lost in the schooner Mary Brown which was wrecked off Queen Charlotte island on her passage down last fall. The hotel is probably the finest building in Alaska. It is furnished with many of the modern improvements, and helps to give the place the appearance of one of those boom towns that used to be seen on Puget Sound a few years ago. No one to-day knows why the hotel was built, not even the company. It is thought that O'Bryon intended establishing a pleasure resort for tourists who would go there to fish and hunt during their summer vacations. In front of the station lies the hull of the old three-masted schooner John Hancock, which was wrecked there several years ago.

The Hancock has quite an interesting history. The gunboat John Hancock was built at Charleston, S. C., in 1846. She was then a side-wheel steamer. After the Mexican war she was transferred to the Pacific coast. She was Commodore Perry's flagship when he negotiated his famous treaty with the emperor of Japan. In later times the Hancock was purchased by Lynde & Hough, of San Francisco, and transformed into a three-masted schooner for the Alaskan trade. Her model was suited for swift sailing, having been very long and slender. She made the quickest passage ever made by a sailing vessel on that route. After she drifted ashore the wreck was filled with rock and a wharf was built out over it.

CHAPTER XXXVIII

Intimately associated with the legend and folk lore of the Indians of Puget Sound is the south wind, the balmy Chinook, the harbinger, the first breath of early spring time. It is the precursor of all that is glorious in pleasant days, sunshine and joy. It comes up over the land, perfumed and odorous from the sea islands. It's touch is like that of a maiden's palm, gentle and soft. Its tread is silent like the flight of a peri, but it is strong in its coming, for snow peaks and icy crags melt before it like banks of fog. It may come in May or it may come in December, and its influence is felt for good. The Indians watch for its coming as they did for the salmon, the king of fishes, long before the white man came upon the coast to share in its benign influence.

There was a beautiful superstition or tradition among the Indians that the Chinook always came in the night time and the white man with all his learning has never yet proved that it does not. The stolid Indian waked in the morning, went to the door of his wigwam and found it fanning his cheeks. The white man came, and he too when he waked himself at morning would find the Chinook a-blowing. So it is to-day. Though the white man has had a half century to discover the secrets of this pleasant wind, they have never yet been told. They only know from whence to look for it — from over the sea — as did the Indians before them.

As all meterologists on the coast know and old residents as well, the prevailing winds of the year are southerly, but all southerly winds are not Chinook blows. They are distinctly different as the vesper and the Dakota blizzard. The Chinook is always a strong, steady southerly wind, never from any other point of the compass, unless it be slightly southwesterly. It is distinctly peculiar to the Northwest Pacific coast and its source is far out in the nasty storm center of the Pacific ocean, emanating from the famed Japan current which is the source of the remarkable humidity of the North Pacific coast.

The Chinook is remarkable for the warming-up it brings, and what is still more singular the glow from its presence is not dependent upon its force. This peculiar wind is, indeed, not a blow in the sense that the word is usually taken, but a smooth, steady flow of a great wind current that is the delight of all who come under its enchanting spell. And what warmth it brings. By official record on the Sound it has been known to elevate the mercury in the thermometer 19 degrees in an hour's time, and yet the Chinook was not blowing above a 12-mile-an-hour rate. That is good evidence that the amount of heat it brings is independent of the force of the wind.

The spring months of the year is the season proper of the Chinook, but meteorologists say there are exceptions and the old and observant pioneer will doubtless bear out this statement. It has been observed to blow in December at Olympia, where is located the oldest weather station in Washington. There 20 years' records of the weather in Western Washington, from a total of 5,700 distinct and separate observations made with a statement of every plus and minus change of 10 degrees or more in both the maximum and minimum of the temperature, shows that the months of the year when the most decided changes

" KLA-HOW-YA "—HOW ARE YOU

occur in Western Washington are March, April, May and October. During the other months the temperature varies but little from day to day. Of decided temperature in this western country 24 degrees is the record of greatest variation in any 24 hours, either of maximum or minimum, that was ever noticed. A change in the maximum of 40 degrees in 24 hours in Texas in winter is said tobe a common thing. The cause is said to be that immediately preceding a norther comes a warm, moist wave, which runs the thermometer up to 65 or 70 degrees on a winter day, and by next morning the thermometer has fallen to 30 or more degrees. By reason of our contiguity to the Japan current such extreme and sudden changes are impossible.

It is only for two months in the year — July and August — that the prevailing winds are not southerly; then they may be said to be northerly. June immediately preceding the first of these two months, and September immediately following them, each have about 50 per cent of northerly and southerly winds.

This mere statement of wind courses is really an explanation of the cause of such a long rainy season on the Northwest coast.   By scientific investigation it has been demonstrated that all cyclonic depressions originating in or over the Pacific ocean during those ten months of the year when southerly winds prevail pass at a sufficiently low latitude to cause the winds in Western Washington to blow from the south or southwest.   These winds always bring up from the ocean that excess of humidity or moistness which is so characteristic of the country.

This prevailing moist-laden atmosphere or wind current from the ocean and the presence of the towering Cascade barrier paralleling the coast so closely is the true secret of the peculiar climate.   Move the Cascade range of mountains and meteorologists tell us that we would at once experience a great difference in climatic conditions.   The excess of moisture now so common on a compara-

SPEARING THE HAIR SEAL

tively narrow strip of coast line would find its way inland and distribute itself over a vast area of country.   Desert and sagebrush plains would be turned into blooming gardens, and corn and wine would grow and flow where now only the sagehen and jack rabbit find congenial homes.   The prevailing south and south-westerly winds would not, say the meteorologists, be interrupted in their regular course because their source would not be interrupted.   And there is so much of that dirty weather always present in the ocean caused by the presence of the Japan current which strikes our coast that the atmosphere would still have its excess of humidity.   In the Japan current lies the source of bad weather off shore and on the coast line.   To such a nicety have meteorologists reduced this potent factor in our weather that they can always with a degree of certainty scarcely attainable in other sections, predict the character of the weather coming on.

CHAPTER XXXIX

Checked by the impenetratable forests that covered all the interior of the country bordering on Puget Sound, the native Indians found pleasure and profit in investigating the marsh lands, tules and tide lands and beaver dams, and chasing the festive musk rat and the industrious beaver; or taking the numerous water fowl by simple methods now forgotten or long in disuse.

Nature for ages had been in process of forming vast tide marshes at the deltas and mouths of the numerous streams, the Duwamish, the Stillaguamish, the Skagit and Nooksack, Puyallup, Skokomish and others. Around the mouths of these rivers many of the largest Indian settlements were to be found. How long these rivers have been silently at work day and night tearing down the mountains and carrying the fragments away to the sea is a question no man can answer. For ages this work has been going on, with results perceptible in the acres of marsh where the rivers meet the tide. If diked and tilled this tide land is the richest and most productive of the whole state for certain kinds of crops.

All hunters know that snipe, ducks and migratory water fowl galore are temporary tenants of these marshy depths every fall and that good sport comes in with the tide at the right season of the year.

At flood tide the "flats" are full of life, for then the little channels that penetrate the tules like a labyrinth are peopled with thousands of gull, ducks, snipe, heron and other water birds, feeding on the crawfish, crabs and other crustacea that dwell in the slimy mud and only come forth when the waters cover the myriads of holes that constitute their homes. Muskrats paddle about towing bits of dead wood or tule in a streaming wake as they take advantage of the tide for water transportation to bring their winter bed to their burrow. Quaint little fellows they are, with beady black eyes that see everything, and a shining coat of brown fur which they oil and comb every time they can find a warm sunny nook where the wind doesn't blow too brisk. They are not very shy if left alone and can often be seen swimming about or perched on some snag smoothing their coat with a little black paw or huddled up until they look like a brown ball of fur as big as your two fists. They have a tireless enemy in the

person of the farmer who owns diked land, for they are the bane of his existence. Dikes seem to be a favorite place for them to dig their burrows in, pre-
sumably because it affords them an elevation above water level, consequently a
dry home in the otherwise slimy expanse of marsh that forms their habitat.

Muskrats are not the only inhabitants of these lonsome, wind-swept deposits.
Gulls wing their circling flight along the borders in quest of food left by the
last tide, and croaking herons rise on heavy, uncertain wing, as they adjust
their lank proportions to the conditions of aerial navigation. The crows are
there always; high tide, low tide or no tide, the crows are about. At low
water they pick up the clams and cockles left on top of the sand, take out the
meat of such as they are able, and have a way of their own of opening those
that persist in keeping their shells tightly closed, On finding one of this kind

INDIAN DUCK HUNTING

they take hold of it with their beak, give a preliminary croak or so, and rise
in the air for several yards, then they drop the clam and follow it like a black
plumb bob to the beach. The clam shell is cracked and mashed by the fall
and the crow has everything his own way by his sharp practices. They clean
up about everything considered eatable in the crow bill of fare that is left on
the beach by the tide and what they miss the gulls get, so that the mud flats constitute a kind of a short order restaurant for the bird-folk that inhabit our bay
shores.

The stoical Siwash stalks, barefooted, over the broad expanse of sand, gathering clams at low tide, or with silent paddle urges his cedar canoe among the
canals of the tule patches, looking for a "pot shot" at ducks with his old
Hudsons bay company musket. He never wastes any powder on a single duck or
risks a wing shot. There must be a whole patch of ducks and they must be close

and sitting still on the water before he turns his old gas-pipe fusee loose in their direction. He don't go for sport, or sportsmanship, this aborigine, so he nearly always gets ducks and generally several of them every time he chucks a double handful of slugs among them.

He is silent as a shadow and piles branches and grass all over his canoe to enable him to do just the right kind of a "sneak" on his unsuspecting victims.

Mrs. Siwash paddles along the canals too, but she is on a peaceful mission and only takes the tules and rushes that grow thick on the tide-flat marshes for no other purpose, in her estimation, than for making mats for her dwelling on the other side of the bay. She knows all the devious windings of every little channel, though some of them are only about wide enough to float her light craft and are hung so close with grass and rushes that you would hardly suspect an open waterway. She knows that this or that blind canal opens out and

KLOOTCHMAN GATHERING RUSHES

gives access to a particularly fine patch of rushes a little further on and urges her boat ahead with lazy stroke that makes it glide along even if there is no water to be seen from your point of view.

These little waterways lead everywhere, and in walking about you find yourself unexpectedly confronted by a ditch a little too wide to jump over and a trifle to deep to wade, when you stop to consider that the bottom mud may be any depth you take a notion to imagine it, but at best deep enough to let the water in over the tops of your waders.

In the deeper ones crabs skurry away in a misfit, sideways fashion, peculiarly their own, and flounders fan their shingle shaped bulk down in the friendly slime and there lie buried as the roil drifts away, conforming so closely with the color of the bottom as to be invisible to any one but a Siwash. They can't fool a Siwash a little bit for he just picks up a spear from his canoe, makes a jab at the muddy spot and eats flounder when he gets hungry.

CHAPTER XL

There's dusky maids
In pinks and plaids,
Maids from the forest free;
   In bright attire,
   Aglow, afire,
On Ballast island by the sea.

There's the chief of his clan
With his ughly klootchman;
The gay young dude and his bride,
   With bows and quiver,
   And dog fish liver,
And the ictas of his curious tribe.

Camped below,
In the beauteous glow,
Such a " gypsy " crew so novel and bold;
   In their long canoes,
   And moccasin shoes,
From the land of the Totem pole.

Dotted all over,
Like pigs in clover,
The wickyups cover Ballast isle;
   Brown flitched salmon,
   Pappooses agammon,
Pots and kettles in curious pile.

When picking's o'er
We'll have no more
The smell that comes from Ballast isle;
   Glad then my eyes
   My spirits rise,
For they've gone back to their paradise.

[Ballast isle is the camping spot near Seattle of the Indians during their stop over to and from the hop fields.]

Hop picking on bright days in the valleys of Western Washington is the delight of the native. It is for him and all his kith and kin, a joy unspeakable. He comes from near and far. He will travel hundreds of miles in his big canim with his full household and all his earthly possessions to enjoy the delightful season as much for his real love for it as for the money that he knows will always come at the close. Then the hop field is redolent of perfume and melody. The fields are alive with pickers; the air is joyous with sound. There is a richness and coloring in the surrounding which form a perpetual delight. There is a novelty to the beholder and a rurality of scene so peculiar, that makes one feel as if they were in some enchanted country. If you have never witnessed a season of hop picking you have missed a rare old time-treat which has its equal only in the maple woods of the East during sugar making time, or in the co'n shuckin' days of old Kentuck, "when the mast am fallin' and the darkies am a singin' and raccoon and possum am simmerin' in the pot."

In addition to its scenic beauties and pleasant surroundings a hop field is a sanitarium for the invalid, and a resting place for the weary and overworked.

Ranking next to the delightful exhilerating smell of the fresh pine woods of Puget Sound is the rich agreeable odor of the hop fields. The hazy half humid air of the lazy September days, the variegated coloring of thousands of native pickers chattering in their gutteral Chinook; the heavy foliaged banks of deep, intensely green fields of vines, with the equally deep green of the conifera woods in the background; the white canvas tents, the lines of curling smoke as-

AN EDUCATED INDIAN

cending heavenward; the half agreeable smell of frying salmon, the universal meal of the brownskinned Indians; the mingling and assimilation of a thousand rural and novel et ceteras, form pictures and attractions seen no where else on earth save in a Washington hop field. They are delights which enjoyed once, never are obliterated from the pleasant memories of the beholder.

There is not a rural panacea or health resort from Southern California to Vancouver island that will afford a tithe of the good solid enjoyment with the revivifying influence so beneficial to constitutions or shattered nerves.

Six o'clock in the morning finds the fields redolent of odor, musical with sound and swarming with pickers. Poles laden with wet vines are falling here, there and everywhere. There are buckets, baskets, boxes, babies and blankets in endless admixture, while white, black and Indian are taking stations. Dropping polls, like snowflakes falling, are heaping in miniature mountains in every row. So it goes. Day in, day out, from morn to night, throughout the season, until the last pole has been plucked and the last load rolled into the mammouth kiln.

Indians make the best pickers, and among the Indians the klootchman ranks supreme. She picks hops while the lazy, indolent brave plays cards or lounges in the shadow of his rakish tepee. His great delights are in card playing and pony racing. Those of the interior will travel for days across the mountains every autumn, not to pick hops but to horse race on Sunday. Sunday is their big day, a day of carousing, gambling and racing. On those days all the villages in the valley are overrun with the pickers in holiday garb of fancy colors. Then assemble a cosmopolitan crowd not greatly unlike such as gather at fair time in the far famed Nijni Novgorod from the steppes of Tartary or Siberia. The Yakimas and Klickitats and other interior tribes, male and female alike, are scampering about on long haired ponies, while the more sedate Puyallups, Nisquallys, Tulalips, and dozens of other coast tribes trudge hither and thither, grunting and muttering and poking their fingers and noses into anything and everything which can be eaten or worn. Night drives them to their various camps, some scattered miles away in various parts of the valleys, and the following Sunday the scene is repeated.

Near Puyallup in a long reach of level ground the Indians have raced for years at hop picking time, and so great is the rivalry and excitement of the sport that

STONE HATCHETS OF PUGET SOUND TRIBES

the whole interim from one autumn till the next is given up in preparation and training of horse flesh with which to outrun rival steeds on the race course. Sometimes but two, at other times six or eight horses will enter in a single race. The race is always a running race and the Indians mount without any reference to weight, handicap, jockey or saddle. A big Indian will be seen mounted on a diminutive wooly pony, and will sail over the course like a meteor, his long black locks streaming in the wind. Bets of ponies, lodges, blankets, saddles, knives, money and everything and anything tangible and movable will be staked on the result of a race and paid with as much nonchalence as a thousand pounds Sterling would be paid on Epsom Downs. Often there are seen at these Sunday races 3,000 people. Such days and places are the paradise of the gambler, contraband whiskey vendor and trashy whites generally. They congregate like vultures at a carrion feed.

Only a goodly number of United States deputy marshals prevents downright and open handed robbery and vice.

The close of the picking season always finds the principal towns flooded with returning pickers and the dock fronts lined with long, lank Indian canoes. The Indians are spendthrifts, and they plant the profits of the picking season as generously as princes of the realm. Their canoes are laden with bric a brac from the Boston man's store as long as the money lasts or as long as there is room to store them.

They always bring with them from their mysterious northern lands the fruits of the chase on land or sea, and the work-manship of rude hands, for barter with the whites. Mats of reeds, images, miniature canoes, bladders of fish oil, slabs of seal meat, dried elk and bear, seal skins, beaver skins, pelts, sea otter skins, and such like, form their chief staples in trade. . These are gen-erally bartered on the trip down, for eatables, while waiting for the maturing of the hop fields, as they are most always here weeks before the time for picking.

QUINIAULT SEA OTTER LOOKOUT

The coast Indians come generally in fleets of a dozen to twenty or thirty big canoes, numbering fifty or one hundred pickers, who are generally presided over by some scion of a royal line or by some head man elected to chieftianship, much as the whites elect their officials. If there is any tribal restrictions or dictatorial authority by the chief at home, it is dropped when they start on their long water journeys, sometimes of many hundred miles, to the hop fields.

The going and coming of the Washington hop pickers is as regular as the annual migration of water fowl or the rotation of the seasons, and are ever a source of attraction and interest.

CHAPTER XLI

The Siwash have a legendary theory and story of the crucifixion. Hezekiah Butterworth picked it up while on one of his vacation jaunts to the west, and tells it very prettily, though it has been told by a score of writers and is one of the first to come to the knowledge of the white man:

Long, long ago, say the Siwashes, in the splended sunsets of the Whulge, or Puget Sea, there came a canoe of copper sailing, sailing. The painted forest lords and feathered maidens saw it from the bluffs — in the sunrise at times, or in the moonsets, but ever in the red sunsets, sailing, sailing. The gleam of copper in the red sunset is more beautiful than gold; and ever and anon on the blue wave was seen the burnished gleam of the copper canoe. On it came, and the solitary voyager in the copper canoe landed at last on the Whulge, under the crystal dome of Mount Rainier, and he shadowed among the cool firs of the headlands there the boat that flashed out the rays of sunset light.

He called together the tribes. They came in canoes from everywhere. He began to teach and preach. "I come among you as a preacher of righteousness," he said, or thoughts like these. "All that men can possess in this world, or any other, is righteousness. If a man have that, he is rich, though he be poor, and his soul shall rise, rise, rise, and live forever.

"Oh Siwashes," he preached, "the unseen power that thinks and causes you to act is the soul. It does not die when the breath vanishes. It goes away with the unseen life and inhabits the life unseen. You have never seen the soul, or life, but death is only the beginning of a longer life, and the soul with righteous longings shall be happy forever.

"But war is wrong—the spear, the arrow, and the spilling of human blood. Man may not kill his brother. The soul was meant for peace."

He preached these or like doctrines, a beautiful gospel, like the Sermon on the Mount.

The warlike tribes rejected the word. They nailed the Saviour who came gleaming over the violet sea in the copper canoe, to a tree, and he died there. They took down his body, but, wonder of wonders! it rose from the dead, and appeared to all the tribes, and the risen Saviour preached the same doctrine of righteousness and immortality as before. The legend may have been derived from the preaching of some forest priest in some distant place, for the Catholic missionaries were on the coast of California before 1700.

Picturesque and profoundly romantic and imaginative is the Siwash legend of the two grand old mountains, Rainier and Hood, one in Washington, one in Oregon, with the mighty Columbia rolling between. It is the legend of a stupendous battle royal, between mighty monarchs, and is as well the sequel to the cascades and rocks that break the broad current of the noble stream. The foundation for the legend is probably due to the fact that within the limits of the Indian tradition or history of the past, Mt. Rainier was in active eruption.

Long ago, almost beyond the time when Indian tradition and legend extend the spirits of the mountains fought a long and bloody battle. Rocks were hurled from the summits at the heads of the rival sentinels of the cascades and a great commotion was caused throughout all the land. The Siwash of the Sound say their tradition teaches them that it was the evil and unruly spirits on Mt. Hood that brought about the great battle. They would not keep still but were bent on raising mischief, and they did it. When the great spirits of Rainier could not stand it any longer and could not sleep, they rose in rebellion with a mighty noise that shook the mountains and the sea and began a war on the noisy demons of Mt. Hood. Great rocks were picked up and hurled back and forth, some so heavy that they could not be thrown the great distance and they fell short landing in the mighty Columbia with a great splash and making the earth tremble from their violence. This quieted the spirits of Mt. Hood, since which they have had peace; but the waters were dammed up and the cascades were formed.

CHAPTER XLII

A long time ago an English whaling bark, after many months of hardship on the voyage, was caught in a heavy gale off Vancouver island coast. After a gallant effort to save the ship and ride out the storm, the captain and crew took to the life-boat, and though a long way from land and with the tempest howling about them, struck bravely out for safety. Nothing was ever heard or seen of the sinking ship. But one of the brave crew reached land to live to tell the awful tale of shipwreck and death which engulfed his companions. It was while trying to make land through the surf of Queen Charlotte sound, that the captain and crew went down. The empty and battered boat was cast upon the shore and with it one half-drowned sailor who, after a time was able to rise from the sand and stagger about.

It was during the stormy winter of 1843, a time long antedating the first general appearance of the settlers. In all the northwest there was scarcely a clearing or hamlet. An occasional white-winged sail dotted the water horizon or came to anchor in some quiet bay or harbor of the Straits of Fuca, or the still less frequented waters of Queen Charlotte sound. Ever and anon a Hudsons Bay company's trapper or voyager emerged from the bush upon the shore to remain a few days and then would be gone again prosecuting his search after skins. That was all there was to the civilization of the inhospitable northwest. The land all about belonged to the simple children of nature the Indian, the beaver and the bear. Such was the situation when the hero of our story was thrown almost drowned upon the beach of Queen Charlotte sound. Scarcely had the half-drowned mariner reached dry land than he was set upon by a party of Indians and taken prisoner. He was escorted to the village of the head chief and the usual council of war held by the braves to determine his fate. The prisoner knew no word of the Chinook jargon or the King George Indian tongue and could not gain the slightest inkling of the drift of the pow-wow. For a time he felt that he was reserved for a fate ten times worse than death at sea, and he cursed fate that he was not permitted to go down with his companions and leave his bones to whiten and bleach in the cavernous depths of old ocean. But he was not to be burned at the stake, nor killed and eaten. The Indians at the close of their council made no demonstration or dangerous move, and he soon learned that he was to remain a prisoner and slave. His English boat was pulled upon the beach and left to rot away. Time passed on and days run into months and months swelled into years. The sailor soon fell into the style of living of the natives and was adopted into the tribe, learned their strange tongue and customs, sat in their councils, went with them on their long canoe voyages to the south and towards the north, followed them in their hunts for the bear, beaver and elk; engaged in their wars with their enemies, dressed in their simple style, and was in every way save by blood an Indian.

For five long years the prisoner lived with his captors on the shores of Queen Charlotte sound, but there came a time when savage life palled and the longing to see the face of a white man and speak his natural language grew too strong to be shaken off. All the time he had lived with the Indians he had not seen a white person. So in 1848 the sailor whose true name was William Jarman, sought an opportunity to escape from the village of his adopted people. He headed his canoe to the south and quickly and quietly paddled away toward the waters of Puget Sound, hoping to fall in with some trapper on the beach, or mayhap catch a sail in the waters towards which he was going. Without mishap he got as far south as Point Wilson, now Point Wilson light house, near Port Townsend, but had the misfortune here to be overtaken by the very people with whom he had lived so long. Broken and bewildered by his recapture, poor Jarman was escorted back to the village in triumphant glee by his swarthy friends, now turned to foes. The policy of the Indians again proved to be to keep him among them as an unwilling prisoner and for four years more Jarman remained a captive and prisoner. Afraid that he would again attempt to escape the Indians took him to Queen Charlotte island, and he was not permitted to return to the main land. Notwithstanding the close surveilance kept upon him the sailor at the end of four years, a second time managed to get away and this time made good his escape. By the time he reached the Sound on his second escape many settlers had arrived and Jarman found company and protection. Such was his wild and uncouth appearance that his later friends gave him the sobriquet of "Blanket Bill." He took up his residence on the Sound, lived at Seattle, Port Townsend and Whatcom, or about the settlements which as time passed on grew to those towns. Blanket Bill after his nine years of wonderful life among the savages never could quite get over the habits and peculiarities he had learned, and consequently he became a notorious character among the white settlers on the Sound. He was living up to a very short time ago somewhere in the bounds of Whatcom county.

www.ingramcontent.com/pod-product-compliance
Lightning Source LLC
Chambersburg PA
CBHW031100280326

41928CB00049B/1187